TEACHING THE
GIFTED IN AN
INCLUSION
CLASSROOM

Activities That Work

Rosemary S. Callard-Szulgit

Rowman & Littlefield Education
Lanham • New York • Toronto • Oxford
2005

This title was originally published by ScarecrowEducation. First Rowman & Littlefield Education edition 2005.

Published in the United States of America
by Rowman & Littlefield Education
A Division of Rowman & Littlefield Publishers, Inc.
A wholly owned subsidiary of The Rowman & Littlefield Publishing Group, Inc.
4501 Forbes Boulevard, Suite 200, Lanham, Maryland 20706
www.rowmaneducation.com

PO Box 317
Oxford
OX2 9RU, UK

British Library Cataloguing in Publication Information Available

Library of Congress Cataloging-in-Publication Data

Callard-Szulgit, Rosemary, 1946–
  Teaching the gifted in an inclusion classroom : activities that work /
Rosemary S. Callard-Szulgit.
      p. cm.
  Includes bibliographical references.
  ISBN 1-57886-185-3 (pbk. : alk. paper)
  1. Gifted children—Education—United States—Handbooks, manuals, etc.
2. Inclusive education—United States—Handbooks, manuals, etc. 3. Activity
programs in education—United States—Handbooks, manuals, etc. I. Title.
LC3993.2.C364 2005
371.95'6—dc22   2004014928

To my husband, Karl Szulgit, who is life, love, spirit, energy, friendship, brilliance, devoted parent, and my one and only, very special love. You have given me everything that could utterly matter in my life: love, caring, children, support, happy times, adventure, support of family and friends, talks, intellectual conversations, travel, financial backing, and professional encouragement—quite simply, all I could have ever asked for and then some. I love you very much and thank you.

CONTENTS

PREFACE

It's just like it happened yesterday. In reality, the event occurred on January 12, 1995. My fourth-grade inclusion classroom was packed with 33 students who were literally tripping over each other in our very crowded space. Twelve children were identified as having ADD and/or ADHD, three were assessed as cognitively gifted, and one was classified as emotionally disturbed. We also had one transfer student whose records had been sealed in second grade. When his transfer records finally arrived three months later, we learned he should have been placed in a sixth-grade classroom. Not only did this transfer student verbally terrorize his fellow classmates, but he urinated on the walls and floor of our classroom bathroom. The paperwork I filled out to document this student's abuse and misplacement in our inclusion classroom filled a folder over two inches thick. After three months, I finally went to the union sobbing and pleading for help.

This classroom was a no-win situation for both the majority of the students and me. I repeatedly begged the principal for help, but in the name of "inclusion" was always sent back to "do my best." I was also scheduled for weekly early-morning CSE special-education meetings in our school. Bear in mind that I was an experienced educator with 28 years of successful teaching under my belt and a specialist in gifted education.

The state of Wyoming sees a drastic decrease in their yearly incidents of misdemeanors upon enacting their new, stiffer penalties.

Courtney Hankins EDU 897

I was putting in between 15 and 18 hours a day on a regular basis, compacting and curriculum differentiating for my students, developing integrated vocabulary lessons, doing required reading records three times a semester for each student, infusing technology into all curriculum areas for my students, and keeping three-week medication "trial" records for three suspected ADHD children.

I wasn't about to give an inordinate amount of additional time to the slower-learning students any more than I could for the gifted children. I refused to "rob Peter to pay Paul." In my mind, to do so would have been completely unacceptable and morally unjust.

Once the union became involved and the superintendent heard about my classroom, a full-time aide was hired and sent in to help me. But it was too late. I bent over to pick up a pencil on the floor one day and couldn't get back up due to severe back pain. I wound up being out of school the remaining four months. A series of five different substitutes was unable to maintain/contain that inclusion classroom, and my terrorizing transfer student was eventually identified as emotionally disturbed and placed in an 8-1-1 classroom.

All in the name of inclusion—my, my, my. Consequently, I have developed this book to help teachers readily access activities designed for gifted students—activities that can work for all.

May it enhance your day and bring you and your students added pleasure. May it ease your daily burdens—and may what happened to me never happen to any other teacher, ever!

INTRODUCTION

Advocates for full inclusion maintain that it is a civil right. One result of the U.S. Department of Education's Individuals with Disabilities Education Act (Public Law 105-17) is the placement of additional numbers of special-education students in our already crowded heterogeneously grouped classrooms. Special-education teachers work in conjunction with classroom teachers, both planning and supporting teaching part-time during the school day.

Stainback and Stainback (1994, 297) state that *full inclusion* is a setting where students with disabilities are served completely within the general-education classroom, with special-education teachers serving entirely as consultants or support personnel. Full inclusion is generally taken to mean that students with mild disabilities can't receive any instruction in "pull-out" settings, such as resource rooms staffed by special-education teachers. All specialized instruction, when needed, is delivered in the general-education classroom by the general-education teacher, special-education teachers, instructional aides, classroom peers, or other support personnel.

What is right with this model? Students identified as special-education students are receiving services from a cadre of professionals: general-education teachers, special-education teachers, aides, peers, and/or other support personnel.

What's wrong with this model? Who is serving the needs of the identified cognitively gifted children in the inclusion classroom? General-education teachers are the primary caregivers in these full-inclusion classrooms, but their load and the classroom responsibilities have already increased with the additional numbers of classified special-education students, not to mention the additional crowding in already crowded regular-education classrooms! Some districts do provide a coordinator for the gifted, but teachers need much more assistance with tasks such as planning, compacting, differentiating, disciplining, monitoring, reporting, and record keeping.

Advocates for education of the gifted maintain that an appropriate and applicable education is also a civil right.

It continues to amaze me when I hear so many citizens espouse the perpetual myths surrounding gifted children and their appropriate education. Few can even say what we really mean when we talk about who the gifted are. The U.S. Department of Education reflects today's knowledge and thinking with the following definition of gifted children as:

> children and youth with outstanding talent who perform or show the potential for performing at remarkably high levels of accomplishment when compared with others of their age, experience, or environment.
>
> These children and youth exhibit high performance capability in intellectual, creative, and/or artistic areas, possess an unusual leadership ca-

pacity, or excel in specific academic fields. They require services or activities not ordinarily provided by the school.

Outstanding talents are present in children and youth from all cultural groups, across all economic strata, and in all areas of human endeavor. (Ross 1993, 26)

Three services/activities that best help in the education of our gifted children are curriculum differentiation, compaction, and acceleration.

Curriculum *differentiation* is a teaching approach that focuses on the higher-level thinking skills of application, synthesis, and evaluation. Teachers respond to where students' mastery levels are, not to grade-level expectations.

With curriculum *compacting*, students may pretest out of units of study they've already mastered earlier in their educational development than their grade-level peers. This gives these students, whose achievement is above grade-level expectations, time to pursue other studies of interest and/or more advanced materials in the curriculum being currently studied.

Acceleration refers to moving students to a level of study that matches their other aptitude and mastery levels in one or more curricular areas. This can be highly effective, especially combined with compacting at the elementary level.

As I mentioned earlier, myths about gifted children and their education continue to abound, not only in the public schools but in private, parochial, and charters schools as well. The following are a few of the more commonly held thoughts regarding education of the gifted—some of which are myths and some reality:

1. **Cooperative learning in heterogeneous groups provides academic benefits for gifted and talented students**.
   Myth: Mixed-ability cooperative learning should be used sparingly for students who are gifted and talented, perhaps only for social-skills development programs. Until evidence is accumulated that this form of cooperative learning provides academic outcomes similar or superior to the various forms of ability grouping, it is important to continue with the grouping practices supported by research.

2. **Acceleration options such as early entrance, grade skipping, early exit, and telescoping tend to be harmful for gifted and talented students**.

Myth: Students who are gifted and talented should be given experiences involving a variety of appropriate acceleration-based options, which may be offered to gifted students as a group or on an individual basis. It is, of course, important to consider the social and psychological adjustment of students for whom such options are being considered, as well as their cognitive capabilities, when making the optimal match to the students' needs.

3. **When using cooperative learning, student achievement disparities within cooperative groups should not be too severe**.
   Reality: When high-, medium-, and low-achieving students are grouped together, high-achieving students explain material to low-achieving students, and medium-achieving students have fewer opportunities for participation. Academically talented students report frustration when working in mixed-ability groups with team members who are unwilling to contribute to the group goal. Placing students who are similar in achievement together continues to allow for heterogeneity in terms of ethnicity and gender in the groups. Cooperative learning might be used with groups of high-achieving students.

4. **Gifted students have lower self-esteem than nongifted students.**
   Myth: The majority of studies seem to indicate somewhat higher levels of general and academic self-esteem for the exceptional group.

5. **Bright, average, and slow youngsters profit from grouping programs that adjust curriculum to the aptitude levels of the groups.**
   Reality: Cross-grade and within-class programs are examples of programs that provide both grouping and curricular adjustment. Children from such grouping programs outperform control children from mixed classes by two to three months on grade-equivalent scales.

6. **In exemplary programs for gifted and talented students, the provision of challenges and choices are major influences on increasing student achievement and motivation.**
   Reality: Themes identified in exemplary gifted and talented programs include: leadership (strong administrative voice to represent and implement the program); atmosphere and environment (supportive, accepting, and positive throughout the school); communication (clear and frequent, between and among parents, teachers, students, and administrators); curriculum and in-

WHO MURDERED THE MINDS OF GIFTED CHILDREN?

PROFESSOR DULL, IN THE CLASSROOM, WITH REPETITIVE DRILLS

struction (teachers' flexibility in matching to student needs); and attention to student needs (commitment to serving students from traditionally underrepresented populations). In addition, the exemplary programs have been found to influence students achievement and motivation through exposure to challenge and choices.

7. **Early reading and writing skills should keep pace with each other.**
   Myth: Contrary to this commonly held belief, there is no relationship between reading and writing skills in the development of talented young children.

8. **Teachers need to show students examples of superior student work in order to challenge them to ever-increasing levels of math achievement.**
   Reality: Talented math students need standards and models. Superior student work can serve to reinforce the development of emerging math skills.

The 2001 law known as the "No Child Left Behind" Act was developed for America's disadvantaged children. It is no secret that many school districts are shifting resources from programs designed for the gifted in order to comply with steady progress toward the 2014 goals of this law. Once again, education for our cognitively gifted takes a hit. However, we do know that what works for the gifted works for all: that inclusive progress rather than an exclusive program is better adapted to community needs, and that all children deserve an applicable and exemplary education as a civil right.

The inclusion classroom certainly has merits, but we simply cannot keep asking teachers to do more and more with less space, less help for the gifted, less help for the regular-education students, less money, less knowledge, and less understanding.

Differentiation brings all students to the synthesis level, the key to personalized learning and its excitement. Differentiation takes time and skill. Through staff development, classroom teachers can be instructed appropriately and have time to work on their curriculum models.

Compacting requires knowledge and continual commitment. It also takes time and skill, which we can give our teachers through the appropriate training and help.

With all the present-day demands on our classroom teachers, including the additional requirements of the inclusion model and activities, it is our moral obligation to remember, serve, and uphold the educational rights of our gifted children and all children.

This book presents some of the best, creative, and educationally appropriate activities I've found for classroom use. Teachers and parents may utilize these activities in the education of their gifted children—and these activities will also work for all students.

Many thanks to my graduate students who kindly shared some of their best activities and ideas as well.

May we all provide the very best education to all students in an inclusion classroom, not just try to survive!

GIFTED BEFORE BREAKFAST, BY JANICE E. MASON

7 a.m.

Shredded Wheat

Morning: I had another dream, only this time I discovered how to balance the budget. But no one would listen to a ten year old. Remember

when I was little and thought if white people had red blood, black people must have green blood? Do newspapers lie? When was the Treaty of Tordesilla signed? My teacher says 1493, but my textbook says 1494. Were all French monarchs named Louis? Why hasn't Pluto been explored? If God had no beginning, He must go so far into the past that He's in the future. Why do we wear matching socks? There's a national flag, bird, anthem, motto. Do nations have a national color? Do mayflies live only a couple of hours for any reason? How were the rings of Saturn formed? Can any chemicals be mixed together to make something sweet? Did you ever notice that houses look like they have faces? Why do some people own a couple of homes, and others don't have any? Do the people in Bosnia and Somalia know anybody cares? Why did we let Hussein go the first time? Is Clinton a good man?

BEEP!!!! BEEP!!!!

I love you, Mom. I don't want anyone I know to get AIDS. How do socks get holes in them? What makes stairs creak? I'd be embarrassed if . . .

8 a.m.

Sigh. The whole world and universe on his shoulder and he can never even remember his lunch!

1

ACCELERATED READER

The award-winning Accelerated Reader is a computerized learning information system for reading and literacy skills. Originally designed for work with the gifted, the technology-based literacy program has demonstrated positive and statistically significant evidence in schools that own it. Accelerated Reader also reports having an especially positive effect on student academic performance for socioeconomically disadvantaged children in urban areas.

The Accelerated Reader is a system of computerized testing and record keeping with a goal of increasing literature-based reading practice. It is also a lifesaver for teachers in test-score and student-record management.

One downside of Accelerated Reader, in my opinion, is that the literature-test questions are geared for the knowledge and comprehension levels of learning and do not really test higher-level thinking skills. However, I can add those questions to the children's learning in small groups or one-on-one conferences.

Overall, I love Accelerated Reader as one more very useful educational tool to use in the classroom.

For further information on Accelerated Reader, please access Renaissance Learning, Inc., at www.renlearn.com.

2

ANGELS IN ACTION

INDIVIDUAL ENTRY

This Georgia-Pacific program designed to reward children who have performed exemplary acts of service to benefit their community, charity, or cause is exactly the type of classroom activity I love to involve my students in. It's applicable to good citizens, community involvement, caring, helping, supporting, and downright kindness! Any adult may fill out the required nomination form, mail it to the address provided by the date listed on the current website, and the nominee may be chosen as one of the *Angel Soft Angels in Action*, with a grand prize of $25,000 and 10 first-place prizes of $2,500. Following are the names and classroom entry activities of the 2003 individual winners.

Sondra Clark, 13, Bellingham, WA

At the age of 11, Sondra had already written two books on encouraging children to volunteer. She also helped raise $65,000 for Childcare International, collected and sent 300 books to Africa, spoken to 100

The descriptions of the 2003 individual and classroom awardees are from "Angels in Action Awards Program," copyright © Georgia Pacific ("GP"). Used with permission. The Angels in Action website is www.angelsoft.com/angelsinaction/.

churches, service clubs, and appeared on 10 television shows sharing her experiences from her work in Africa.

Kristina & Liza Giangrande, 10 & 8, Andover, MA

In 2000, Kristina and Liza started a hat and mitten drive for neighbors in need, raising $18,000 worth of clothing. In 2002, the girls expanded the drive and raised $27,000 worth of new clothes that were distributed to over 1,000 needy schoolchildren.

Anna Goddu, 15, New York, NY

Over the past two years, Anna has created a series of classes called DTK, Digital Technology for Kids. In these classes, East Harlem students learn about digital technology programs. To help get the classes started, Anna applied for grant money and designed lesson plans. Anna is currently designing a video instruction class so 10th graders can produce a video about their school.

Devon Green, 12, Stuart, FL

Devon started a recycling business when she was five and now recycles for more than 100 businesses. She coordinated her own campaigns to raise more than $70,000 for The Hibiscus Children's Center, a shelter for abused and neglected children. In addition, Devon raised $16,500 and two tons of pet food for the Humane Society. She is currently on a "lecture tour" to discuss her experience.

Colleen Judge, 13, Dayton, OH

This year, Colleen is gearing up for the fourth annual Concert of the Giving Strings Orchestra, an organization this young cellist and pianist founded in 2000. Money raised from the concert is donated to several different children's charities.

Jacob Komar, 11, Burlington, CT

Devoted to helping underprivileged kids get ahead in school, Jacob started "Computer for Communities" when he was just nine years old.

He took a garage full of old computers, updated and rebuilt them, obtained software licensing, and enlisted the Department of Social Services to distribute them to families in need. Today, companies and schools make donations and Jacob has given away more than 60 computers and has taught more than 140 kids how to use them.

Anthony Leanna, 11, Suamico, WI

Anthony started "Heavenly Hats" to collect hats for cancer patients who lose their hair due to treatments. He has collected more than 8,000 hats, which he has donated to more than 60 hospitals throughout the United States.

Daniel & Elizabeth Nally, 15 & 13, Westwood, MA

In 1996, after hearing about a shortage of turkeys for Thanksgiving, this sister and brother team started an organization called "Turkeys 'R' Us." They are nationally recognized and have helped feed over 500,000 needy people. Because of their program, there is now a "Turkeys 'R' Us" in Chicago and a nationwide school project called the Turkey Challenge Cup.

Brant Whiting, 11, Fullerton, CA

To promote the benefits and joys of reading, Brant established the "Read All Over" program that donates used children's books to classroom libraries. Through his program, more than 2,200 books have been collected to date. There has also been a website established to help facilitate the donation of books.

Ruben Ybarra, Jr., 11, Superior, AZ

Ruben spent months creating and organizing the first annual "Cystic Fibrosis Bubble Gum Blow-Off" and is working to grow it into a fundraising event to be held in cooperation with public schools nationwide. Prizes were solicited by local businesses and 25 percent of the money raised was given to Superior's budget-slashed schools.

Angel Soft® Angels in Action®

Certificate of Achievement

Awarded To:

**Eugenia
from Rochester**

For the significant achievement of:

**Introduced Dr. Rosemary Callard-Szulgit and her two
books on gifted education and children to the
Chinese Community School parents.**

October 11, 2003
DATE

*Angel
Soft*

A

GROUP ENTRY

Any teacher in grades 3–8 whose class is making a difference in their community may submit a nomination to recognize his or her "angelic" students for their good deeds. The required nomination form must be mailed by the date listed on the most current website entry form. The grand prize is $10,000 cash for the school of the winning classroom for school purposes and $1,000 for the teacher of the winning class. Following are the 2003 classroom contest winner and finalists.

The Stadium School (Grade 7 & 8), Baltimore, MD (winner)

Students started a group called "Youth Dreamers" that is working to create a youth-run community center for teens to go to after school as an alternative to loitering or being recruited to gangs. They have put in over 300 hours of service, raised more than $200,000, have written grants, and have generated local media coverage.

Addison Elementary (Grade 4), Marietta, GA

Students forged relationships with senior citizens through monthly interviews and activities. Through this, students were able to capture the seniors' life stories and wrote them in their own books, which were later professionally published and given to the seniors.

Birmingham Elementary School (Grades 3–6), Toledo, OH

As part of the curriculum, students attend "MicroTime" studies, a class where they apply in-class learning to "real-life" situations. Through Angels in the Classroom, teachers recognized that volunteerism should be part of the learning experience. Therefore, MicroTime classes began weekly service projects including: creating placemats for soup kitchens, developing hygiene kits, making cards for armed services, and organizing school cleanups.

Colonia Middle School (Grades 5–8), Colonia, NJ

Students designed a program called "Kids for Kindness." They adopt a grandparent at a local home and participate in intergenerational activities, such as Senior Prom, bingo, and Adopt-A-Grandparent.

Field Middle School (Grades 5 & 6), Minneapolis, MN

Local pet shelters had an overcrowding problem since many people in the community abandoned their pets because they couldn't afford pet food. To help solve this problem, Field students partnered with local food shelters and organized a pet food drive. Students wrote flyers, distributed notices and newsletters, and sent e-mails to help promote the drive.

Grover Cleveland Middle School (Grade 7), Dorchester, MA

Grover Cleveland's "Teens Keeping It Real" (TKIR) is a volunteer program created by kids for kids to provide and encourage volunteer opportunities for Grover Cleveland students. This year's TKIR program consists of four different opportunities: a coat and can drive, a mentor/tutor program, garden planting, and making Thanksgiving dinner for local needy families.

Liberty Elementary School (Grade 4), Port Charles, FL

For the past four years, the class planned and hosted an event called "Empty Bowls" to help raise awareness of the homeless problem in the area. Students made ceramic bowls and asked local businesses for donations to purchase soup for $10 each. They raised $5,000, which they used to help build the county's first homeless shelter.

Moraine Community School (Grade 6), Moraine, OH

Students developed "Operation Green Space." Each student spent a minimum of 20–50 hours creating at least one "green space"—an asphalt area turned into a green oasis by planting grass, trees, plants, and shrubs.

Otis Brown Elementary School (Grade 4), Irving, TX

The students collected eyeglasses to be donated to needy people. To raise awareness of the program, they created mailers, developed flyers, and distributed schoolwide announcements. Over 900 pairs of eyeglasses were collected and donated.

Robert Mascenik Elementary (Grade 5), Iselin, NJ

Students designed a program called "5th Grades Care." They collected gently used shoes, coats, and specialty items and donated them to various shelters. Each month, they choose a new product or clothing item to collect for the homeless or needy in their community.

Sunnyside Elementary (Grade 4), Bonita, CA

The "Kids Giving Kids" program was created to memorialize two Sunnyside students who lost their battles with cancer. Students have raised more than $43,000 to donate to the Children's Hospital of San

Diego (where children are treated for cancer), as well as more than $14,000 in other donations such as toys and clothes.

Windy Ridge School (Grades 6 & 8), Orlando, FL

Students worked together to help 1st-grade, disadvantaged kids learn to read. To date, the students have spent 360 hours of their time teaching the younger children, with each child volunteering 40 minutes a day. The program also resulted in a 90 percent improvement rate in the 1st-grade students' reading.

Wooster Middle School (Grade 7), Stratford, CT

A group of 128 students made it their goal to help the local homeless population. They gathered 3,000 toiletries, triple their initial goal. In addition, they collected stuffed animals for abused or lost children and socks for an area rescue mission.

At any time, simply go to the Internet at www.angelsoft.com/angelsinaction/ for the latest information and contest rules.

Angels in Action is a perfect type of program support we need in our schools to encourage kids to start their own community service projects—and how wonderful it is to identify our very own individual angels right in our classrooms!

Georgia-Pacific also makes an Angel Soft Angels in Action Kit available for order at a nominal fee off the website. The kit includes:

- A 12-month motivational calendar with 60 inspirational stickers
- A student activity guide to get your child started
- A parent guide full of helpful advice

Certificates are also available on the Angel Soft website for adults to use for children, students, and other adults they would like to recognize for angelic accomplishments. I used one as a thank you to Eugenia Chen for introducing me and my first book, *Parenting and Teaching the Gifted* (2003a) School, to the Chinese Community School of Rochester.

Angels in Action also provides overview letters to students, parents, and teachers as follows:

Dear Student:

Ser-vice \ n: the act of serving as a helpful act; a good turn.

The Angel Soft® Angels in Action® Program is all about getting kids like you involved in service projects that help their communities. In this section of the website, you'll find plenty of ways to come up with project ideas and make them happen.

So what are you waiting for? Put your ideas into action!

Dear Parent:

Engaging in community service with your child can be a fulfilling and bonding experience as a person and parent. By showing the importance of giving back to others, you demonstrate what it means to be a responsible citizen, good neighbor, and community leader.

What's more, volunteering can be fun! And, volunteering can have a positive, lasting effect. Studies show that community service helps increase a child's confidence, responsibility, compassion, and self-esteem—all benefits they'll enjoy for a lifetime.

In this section of the site, we'll show you how you and your child can work to start simple, think big, and make a difference in your community and the world around you.

Dear Teacher:

Across the nation, more and more young people are making meaningful contributions to their communities. And as a teacher, your example helps keep this trend going by building character and leadership skills in your students. What you do each day helps to shape your students into thoughtful neighbors and civic leaders.

That's where the Angel Soft® Angels in Action® In-School Program comes in. As part of the national Angel Soft® Angels in Action® program, we're offering teachers the opportunity to take advantage of two key components: a comprehensive service learning toolkit and the chance to win $10,000 for your school!

The purpose of the Teacher's Guide is to provide you with the tools you need to lead your class in development and execution of a community service project. Have fun with this program! Use this guide in the best way you see fit—and feel free to choose those exercises that you think will keep your students motivated. As a result, your students will learn that doing good can be good fun . . . and can win $10,000 for their school.

The actions your students take today will benefit them and their communities for years to come. We hope this program helps start your students on a lifetime of community involvement. We applaud you for your commitment to your students and the community.

Since I first heard about these Angels in Action Contests, I have exposed more than 200 of my graduate students and educational colleagues. I eagerly await hearing about one of their students and/or classrooms winning. I'll be just as happy to hear that one of my readers, students, and/or classrooms won as well. Please e-mail me at szulgit2@aol.com with your happy news!

3

BRAINSTORMING

I'll never forget my first official encounter with brainstorming. It was my fifth year as a professional educator in 1973. I had been selected to be an administrative intern at our District Office. Eager, bright-eyed, and bushy-tailed, I was ready to conquer the world with creativity, innovation, and life-challenging lessons.

We had assembled around a beautiful oak table on a Friday morning in the boardroom. Our superintendent had put up a district problem on the front board, asking all of us at the meeting to brainstorm solutions. The one rule everyone seemed quite aware of was that wild ideas are encouraged in the brainstorming process. "Piggybacking" is another rule of brainstorming.

I have never been at a loss for ideas. Creative thinking has always been relatively easy for me. In fact, while most educators encourage thinking "out of the box," administrators usually wanted me to get "back into the box" throughout my career.

At first, when my colleagues started voicing outrageous ideas, in my mind, I thought, "How utterly stupid!" I couldn't imagine why anyone would want to piggyback on any of the "ridiculous" suggestions listed on the blackboard. As one of life's "learning lessons" would have it, however, 20 minutes later, my brain clicked onto one of the absurd ideas I had duly noted in my mind earlier, and I came up with the idea that everyone agreed would be workable and valuable for the district. Since that day, I understand and value brainstorming.

Three differentiating characteristics of creative children are:

- They have a reputation for wild and silly ideas.
- Their productions tend to be off the beaten track.
- Their work is characterized by humor and playfulness.

A stimulating activity to introduce brainstorming is to instruct the class to write the names of the Seven Dwarfs and the Seven Wonders of the World without speaking aloud. When no one student gets the entire list, ask who has six or five. Have others fill in the lists to emphasize that group thinking is more productive.

The group problem-solving technique of brainstorming follows four ground rules (Dickinson, Dickinson, and Rideout 1987, 7):

1. Withhold judgment of ideas: An essential problem-solving skill is the ability to conceptualize freely. Conceptualization is the process that creates ideas. A judgmental attitude would cause group members to be more concerned with defending ideas than generating them.
2. Encourage wild ideas: It is easier to tame down an idea than to think one up.
3. Quantity counts: The more creative ideas one has to choose from, the better.
4. Piggyback on the ideas of others: Participants are encouraged to build on or modify the ideas put forth by other group members.

As a freewheeling group activity, brainstorming promotes positive reactions and instantaneous imagination. I wholeheartedly encourage my graduate students to teach and use brainstorming in their own classrooms. It truly is a wonderful group-thinking activity that always winds up with positive, useful, and agreed-on ideas.

I recommend the book *Brainstorming Activities for Creative Thinking*, by C. Dickinson, P. Dickinson, and E. Rideout (1987), which contains more than 100 pages of 3-, 5-, and 15-minute brainstorming activities you can use to teach this problem-solving activity to your students. You'll all stretch your creative minds, reach positive answers, and have fun doing these sessions together!

(4)

BRINGING SHAKESPEARE'S METER ALIVE

Kristen Petitti

Rationale. Many ask why English teachers still feel compelled to teach Shakespeare in their classrooms. I find Shakespeare's intricate tangling of plots, outstanding development of conflict within these plots, and unforgettable characters to be timeless exemplars of literature. While students can understand my enthusiasm about these elements, they cannot always see a difference between what Shakespeare does and how other authors use these elements for themselves. A more concrete way to show Shakespeare's genius is to teach meter and his use of iambic pentameter. Then students can appreciate his creativity and ability to manipulate language in a way very few writers can. The problem still stands, however: How can I make 14-year-olds understand the complexity of meter?

Step 1: Understand that writing can have a rhythm just like music (introduce Dr. Seuss). Have students clear a large space on the classroom floor. They will stand in a circle, each facing the back of the person in front of them. As you read *Horton Hears a Who*, stress every other syllable. When you begin reading, have the students march in a circle. They will stomp loudly when you stress a syllable and softly when you read an unstressed syllable. Begin *slowly* until students understand the process, then gradually speed up. After completing a line smoothly, ask the students to sit back at their desks, which are arranged in a circle along the outside of the room.

Step 2: Talk about writing and rhythm. Ask the students questions leading to the connection that Dr. Seuss books have rhythm, much like musical rhythm. Such leading questions could be:

- What did you feel while marching?
- How did it sound when everyone was marching?
- When reading Dr. Seuss books, what do you notice about the sound of the story?
- How is this like music?

Step 3: Introduce vocabulary words for meter and its functions. Explain that the reason a book can sound this way is that it has a rhythm, and this rhythm is called *meter*. At this point, read from notes on what meter is.

Step 4: Make meter come alive through "bongo drums." As you explain each type of foot, use your hands on the desk like bongo drums to show the sound each meter makes. The students can mimic your pounding. Then discuss the words that describe how many feet are in a line. Relate these words to math words: for example, a *hex*agon has six sides and a *hex*ameter is six feet in a line.

Step 5: Illustrate Shakespeare's expertise. Explain to students that Shakespeare wrote his plays completely in iambic pentameter, breaking meter only in certain situations that you can discuss later (for example, plebians spoke in prose to show lower-class rank). The students will often say this is impossible, so ask them to open to any page in *Romeo and Juliet* and find an exception. Let one student choose a line that you can use. Place it on a large chalkboard with the stressed syllables written in capital letters and the unstressed syllables written in lowercase letters. Then ask for 10 volunteers to stand under the syllables. The rest of the class must read the line on the board as the stressed-syllable people rise to their toes and yell their words. The unstressed-syllable people will duck down and whisper their words. Read the line like this until fluidity is achieved. At this point, the students will understand meter!

5

THE CALLARD-SZULGIT
STAR OF EXCELLENCE

I started putting my "Callard-Szulgit Star of Excellence" on children's papers almost 15 years ago. I just splashed one on Doug's paper one day, covering his entire page. From that point on, everyone wanted a Callard-Szulgit star. This was in a 4th-grade classroom. Grades actually improved as kids become more careful with their work so they could obtain one. Children at every grade level loved them.

Smiles increased, too, and the stars were even a hit in middle school—really! I've never underestimated the power of positive reinforcement—and a splash of boldness. Hey, whatever works!

6

CLOZE

In the early 1990s, American schools became heavily involved with CLOZE activities and testing. CLOZE techniques were developed to build and improve reading understanding—reading for meaning. I liked CLOZE paragraphs and approached the activities with my students in a modified SQ3R Format. CLOZE helped children focus, read with a purpose, increase and improve their vocabulary, and increase reading comprehension scores. Currently, the educational pendulum has swung away from CLOZE. I personally think we should bring it back and use it as one more activity to improve student achievement.

Here's an example of a CLOZE activity (Cimochowski 1993, 9): Hippocrates, who lived in ancient Greece, studied the bodies of human beings and looked for natural causes of disease. He established a pledge for proper conduct of _____. This pledge, known as the Hippocratic Oath, is still followed by medical doctors today.

The possible answers are: a) Americans, b) students, c) governments, d) physicians, and e) children. The answer is d) physicians.

7

CREATIVE PROBLEM SOLVING (CPS)

Every semester I teach EDI 651, "Teaching the Gifted, K–12," I emphatically tell my graduate students that if there is one other very important thing to do besides taking all students to the synthesis/evaluation level of Bloom's taxonomy, it is to teach creative problem solving (CPS) to their children and actively use this model throughout the year.

Eberle and Stanish (1985, 12) state that creative problem solving is a basic skill and a good-sense approach to modern-day living and learning. It is a practical style of learning having transfer value. It is also a model for improving relationships, dealing with social uncertainties, and reducing stress that individuals sometimes experience. I absolutely agree. I have been using CPS for over two decades with my students, ages 6 to 60+.

Just this past semester, one of my full-time graduate students (Sue) had a best friend (Julie) who was a first-year teacher in a small town in downstate New York. Julie was faltering due to the lack of discipline and common courtesy of students in her classroom. For her final creativity project in our course, Sue drove 150 miles and spent a day with Julie and her unruly students. Sue presented the CPS model to them all. Together, they worked out a positive and acceptable solution for better behavior.

Was Sue's day with Julie and her unruly students successful? YES! YES! YES! YES!

When Sue presented her "creativity project" to our class, she also read all the wonderful thank-you notes she had received from the first-graders, along with a tear-jerking letter from her best friend. I just love it when students and teachers make learning applicable to life! Yahoo!

CPS follows a six-step method, and each step of the problem-solving scheme has a distinct purpose. The steps are interrelated, with one step leading to the next (Eberle and Stanish 1985, 13–14).

STEPPING THE LEVELS OF CREATIVE PROBLEM SOLVING

Level 1: Sensing Problem and Challenges

- Being alert to situations and conditions needing improvement.
- Noticing and getting the feeling that things are not as good as they should be.

Level 2: Fact Finding

- Getting information as an aid to understanding the situation.
- Asking questions, digging in, and getting at the cause of things.

Level 3: Problem Finding

- Looking at the whole puzzle to see how the pieces fit together.
- Selecting and stating a manageable problem.

Level 4: Idea Finding

- Coming up with lots of ways to solve a problem.
- Thinking up things that nobody else will think of.

Level 5: Solution Finding

- Looking at our ideas to see which one might work.
- Picking out the ideas that measure out as best.

Level 6: Acceptance Finding

- Preparing a plan to put our ideas to work.
- Figuring out what needs to be done and how to do it.

Creative problem solving can and should be taught. I promise you'll be amazed at the extremely positive results you and your students will achieve as a result of teaching and using CPS.

Bob Eberle and Bob Stanish provide a book chock full of exemplary lessons for each of the six steps in creative problem solving in *CPS for Kids: A Resource Book for Teaching Creative Problem Solving to Children*. Purchasing this book will be money very well spent, truly!

P.S. Sue earned an A+ on her creativity project assignment.

8

DIVERSITY OF LIFE

Greg K. Szulgit

OVERVIEW

Diversity of Life is a fully prepared exercise that teaches principles of biodiversity and ecology by incorporating science, math, and language skills. It is a fun outdoor game in which students, pretending to be uniquely adapted creatures, scramble for nutritional resources in different environments. They then record their successes and shortcomings on their data tables to be tallied up in the classroom. The accompanying worksheets challenge students (and teachers) to ask critical thinking questions about biodiversity in both the game and the real world. It is pitched at the 4th- to 6th-grade levels, but can be easily adapted for any level of student (it's even been used successfully with undergraduates at San Diego State University). Teachers need only supply some kitchen utensils (plastic cutlery will do), paper cups, and some dry cereal or macaroni.

Objective

To get students thinking about biodiversity and ecological principles, and to incorporate math and language into a fun exercise.

Lesson Time

Approximately 1 hour (or more if desired)

Requirements

- a few different types of small, biodegradable particles of varying sizes (e.g., dry macaroni, cooked spaghetti, peas, green beans, peanuts, chopped apples, tree leaves, etc.)
- several kitchen utensils and/or simple tools (use discretion with younger ages)
- paper cups

Ages

Any age (primary through college)

Summary

1. The teacher will scatter food particles over an outdoor area.
2. Students will pick up food particles, using only their utensils, for one minute.
3. Students will tally their particles.
4. The game is repeated with a predator and safety zones.
5. Results are discussed in the classroom (reports can follow if desired).

Details

1. Lay a large number of kitchen utensils (and/or simple tools, depending on age) out on a table or the floor (plastic forks and spoons are an inexpensive addition to fancier utensils such as hamburger tongs, beach shovels, and colanders). Hand out paper cups. Explain the game to the class and have each student choose a utensil that will be their "mouthpart" as they metamorphose into a new creature.
2. Select an outdoor area that has at least two different terrains (e.g., pavement, grass, and dirt) and scatter food particles over

the area. It helps to have at least three types of very different particles (e.g., some that can be stuck with forks such as apple chunks, hard food such as peanuts, and slimy food such as cooked spaghetti). *Note: This step is actually best done ahead of time, but birds may eat your food particles unless you have a person acting as a scarecrow.*

3. Give the students one minute to gather as much food as they can using *only* their chosen utensil (have them hold their paper cups by biting the edges; this prevents use of the cup as a tool and also drastically reduces the noise level).

4. Students return to the teacher and tally (on paper) their results. The student with the lowest yield has starved to death and comes back in the next round as a predator.

5. Establish two safety zones where the creatures (students) are free from attack by the predator (students can touch an object such as a slide or a wall). Repeat the game. Any creature that the predator catches is dead. In addition, the creature with the lowest food yield starves. The game can be repeated several times, but twice is usually enough. Return to classroom.

6. Write down the category of utensil on the board and tally the numbers for each student. This is a great opportunity to teach the basic statistical concept of the "average" (don't let them get intimidated; if they can add and divide, they can find an average).

Interesting Things to Think About
(including cool* words that follow)

1. Creatures are very *diverse** in their shapes, sizes, and *appendages.**
   a. Why do you think different creatures have different mouthparts?
   b. Think of the mouthpart that you had during the Diversity of Life game. What is a creature in the natural world that has a mouthpart similar to the one that you had?
   c. Where does this creature *forage** and what does it eat?
2. Competition for food and *predation** are both *selective pressures.**
   a. How did the presence of a predator affect your foraging in the second round as compared with the first round?

Jeff Siuda '03

    b. What strategies did you use to avoid predation (did you run fast? did you hide? did you travel within a group?).

3. Different creatures take advantage of different *niches.**

    a. The mouthpart that you had might have been more useful for collecting one type of food than another. What was the most common food type that you collected?

    b. What *terrain** was easiest for you to forage in? (Was it grass? dirt? pavement? etc.)

    c. If you combine characteristics of your foraging, you can start to describe the special niche that you adapted to. For example, if you collected mostly dry macaroni and mostly from the pavement, then you took advantage of the "dry macaroni/pavement" niche. What niche did you take advantage of? Did others with the same mouthparts do the same?

    d. Consider the type of mouthpart that did the *least* well in the game. Can you think of a niche in which it would do *most* well (it does not have to be one that was available during the game)? What would it be? Hint: think of an animal that has a similar mouthpart in the natural world and think of where it forages.

*Cool Words

appendage: an external organ or limb

diverse: capable of various different forms

forage: to search for food or provisions

niche: the specific combination of factors used by an organism to exist in an environment

predation: the consumption of one creature (the prey) by another (the predator)

selective pressure: any factor that prevents the reproduction of those creatures that do not meet a certain criteria (in other words: selective pressure kills those that can't forage)

terrain: a region of the ground that is different than the other regions around it

9

FINDING FORRESTER

Two days after I was hired to teach the graduate course EDI 648, "Teaching Writing, K–12," my husband and I happened to rent the video *Finding Forrester*. We were enthralled with the creative and powerful teaching dynamic(s) Sean Connery portrayed as the Nobel Prize–winning novelist, William Forrester.

I was so excited I could barely contain myself. I knew viewing and discussing this film would be a wonderfully creative assignment for my graduate students. As an educator, I have a continual goal: to provide my students with plenty of "thinking" exercises and conversations (as well as projects) throughout the courses.

This is my fourth year of teaching this writing course to graduate students. I can unabashedly say that including *Finding Forrester* has revolutionized the thinking of my students. They continually report back to me and their classmates how their own students are more free to create and think in their writing with their hearts first.

Following are some examples and excerpts from graduate *Finding Forrester* overviews my own students wrote for class.

The Writing Process: One Size Does NOT Fit All!

C. Holzschuh '03

FINDING FORRESTER RESPONSES

"As I reflect on the movie and the different writing styles that were addressed, it allowed me to realize that writing is a gift and one of the most wonderful talents that an individual may possess."

—Marcy Marino

"The relationship between William and Jamal is one that every teacher should strive to attain with their students."

—Tricia Ike

"My favorite party of the movie was when Mr. Forrester told Jamal, 'There is black and there is white . . . your writing should be full of color.'"

—Heidi Zwetsch

"Finding Forrester has to be one of the most powerful movies ever!
I have seen it several times, I actually own a copy now, and never tire
of watching the drama unfold as mentor and students grow in their
individual existences."

—Jessica Kenyon

"Gus Van Sant's *Finding Forrester* is a touching film that offers much
to think about the crafts of writing and friendship. In terms of writing, William Forrester (Sean Connery) is an advocate for the idea
that writing is primarily an avenue for emotional release, an impul-
sive act unmediated (at least at first) by reason. He thus encourages
his young pupil, Jamal Wallace (Rob Brown), to give himself over to
the rhythm of the typewriter keys, explaining that '[y]ou write your
first draft with your heart and you rewrite with your head. The first
key to writing is to write, not to think.' Given that most teenagers
who write on a regular basis view their journals or diaries as arenas
in which to sort out their roiling adolescent emotions, this is astute
advice on Forrester's part.

Coupled with this 'heart-first, head-second' philosophy is Forrester's belief that writing is a deeply personal act. His own landmark
novel, for instance, treads on sensitive ground, and he is resentful of
commentators who have sullied his and his brother's experiences
with their own interpretations: 'I didn't write [*Avalon Landing*] for
[the critics]. . . . And when [they] started all this bullshit about what
it was I was really trying to say. . . . Well, I decided then, one book
was enough.' At first, it seems that Jamal is the perfect audience for
such a sentiment. After all, he too is intensely secretive about his
writing, composing late at night or furtively scribbling when inspira-
tion strikes between classes at his inner-city high school. What both
characters ultimately learn, though, is that one cannot deny the com-
municative aspect of writing. The lesson of *Finding Forrester* is that
writing is, fundamentally, a social act—that being a writer makes you
more a part of the world, not someone who can hide from it. When
a person writes, a compact is forged between two individuals: the
writer promises to share authentic experience, while the reader vows
to both respect the writer's perspective and use those ideas to fuel
further experiences and, hopefully, written reflections of his/her
own. And the cycle continues.

As one would imagine, being a high school English teacher
blessed and cursed with the task of drawing written expression from

the hearts and minds of 16-year-old boys, I found *Finding Forrester* to be very inspiring, partly because it affirms much of what I already do. I constantly encourage my students to begin their writing processes by turning off their inner critics and allowing themselves to get carried away in a stream of ink. To that end, we begin almost every class with an automatic or free write exercise. I put a provocative phrase or question on the board, and the boys have 5 minutes to respond. The only rule is that their pens must never stop moving; even if they briefly lapse into gibberish, they must not stop their hands from sliding across the page. At the end of the 5 minutes, students have the option to share their creations, and I will occasionally ask that they turn one of these paragraphs into more formal pieces. My hope is that the students discover that the physical act of writing can prompt thought, that you sometimes cannot learn what it is you know or believe without, as Forrester puts it, 'punching the keys.'

The film has also given me much to think about in regards to literary interpretation. As the school year chugs along, I sometimes catch myself treating works of literature as puzzles that my students and I have to solve. *Finding Forrester* is an excellent reminder that novels, short stories, poems, and plays are created by fallible human beings who may be deeply conflicted about what they produce and do not simply exist to keep English teachers in business. Not everything in a work of literature has to mean something; sometimes it just is, to be treasured, not decoded."

—Jeff Sinda

"What a way to learn to write—from a master writer himself. This movie challenges the way that every English teacher drills students to write. The irony is that the movie challenges something many of us believe is wrong anyway, but practical. Thesis statements, topic sentences, grammar, outlines, and the writing process take over our classes as we attempt to teach students how to write, to systematically teach every child the same thing, and to have a way to grade that child's writing.

Although we know the 'art' of writing is often massacred in our classrooms by deadlines and standards, we frequently feel unable to protect the appreciation of such an art. *Finding Forrester* breaks the rules of writing since 'a lot [of people] know the rules of writing, but they can't write.' The style of writing demonstrated, not taught, in this film is one where writing breaks structure to first write what is in the heart. Forrester instructs his young student to 'write.' He claims that the key to writing is to write, not think. Get everything onto paper that is from the heart in the first draft; then, enjoy the greatest moment—reading your first draft alone—before anyone can critique it. Once your heart is out, write your second draft with your head. How simple. How simple?

Why is it that we, as educators of our language, do not do this for our young students? I know that not every student learns to write or can write in the same manner. But I teach them all similar writing processes regardless because I feel that I don't have the time to do otherwise. I grade what they write and they never just write. My style in the classroom is agreed on as the mode of teaching writing for too many of us. I wonder how many writers like Jamal have been stifled by these teaching methods. Could one be sitting in front of me every day? I always (as I believe many educators do) dream of being that teacher that really teaches a love for reading and writing for some students; but I often find inspirational works, such as this movie, that awaken me to the fact that I must do something out of the humdrum of normalcy to have such an influence. Why can't students write as a form of self-expression or enjoyment merely for self-expression and enjoyment? I think they should, and I am the one (gladly) obliged to give them that opportunity."

—Kristen Petitti

"'Heart.' That's the one word that comes to mind when I think of the movie *Finding Forrester*. 'The first draft you write with your heart; the second with your head,' William Forrester advised Jamal Wallace in the screenplay's most memorable line. As a pianist's heart is to his/her playing, so is a writer's heart to his/her composing. I thought that *Finding Forrester* captured the two extreme approaches to writing and the teaching of writing (one heartfelt and one heartless) very well. In its didactic theme, it reminded me that writing and writing instruction done by the intellect alone will never be as powerful as writing and writing instruction done through the heart. I agree with every aspect of Forrester's way, which the film endorses.

William Forrester's writing style and style of teaching writing both contrast with that of Robert Crawford's. Forrester's compositions are lively, fresh, easy, spontaneous, genuine, private, and written to please himself first; Crawford's words are full, stale, pedantic, laborious, artificial, and calculated to please the public. Forrester discredits 'coffee-shop reading shit' as fakery; conversely, Crawford is

the chairperson of the school writing competition, with its public reading requirement.

The teaching of writing is an extension of our own writing process, as the film shows. Forrester's instructional methods are positive, confident, and respectful, helping to produce student writing that expresses the writer. In a cozy environment, his home, Forrester pushes Jamal into the energetic rhythm of typing and passionately praises him: 'Punch those keys! . . . Now you've got it!' Forrester disregards hard-and-fast rules of grammar and teaches Jamal to take risks with his writing. Forrester's teaching style is stress-reducing. He believes in mentoring and guiding. He forms a close, personal bond with his student, building him up so the writing process can be meaningful. In everything he does, Forrester uses his heart.

Crawford's instructional methods, on the other hand, are negative, hesitant, and disrespectful, confining the student's writing in fear of what harsh critics like he will say. In an intimidating environment, the elitist school, he regards Jamal's writing suspiciously, warns him to tread lightly, and threatens him with academic punishment. Crawford is the guru of silly grammar rules, and he paralyzes Jamal with fear of failure. Crawford's style is stress-inducing. He believes in being condescending and dictating. He alienates himself from his students, tearing them down so the writing process is meaningless. In everything he does, Crawford uses his (misguided) head only.

More than just advocating one writing or teaching style over the other, the movie presents writing as a magic tool for gaining insight into the human condition. Young, black Jamal and old, white Forrester are kindred spirits because (1) they share a love of reading and writing and (2) they have each experienced the trauma of losing family. They both realize that writing is useful to them in understanding their reactions and processing their pain. They have given themselves 'the write therapy.' Writing is effective work on the self; it helps us 'find ourselves'; hence the movie's metaphorical title, *Finding Forrester*. With the fresh blood from Jamal's innocent heart infusing his cripped veins, Forrester rediscovers himself after decades of being lost in a deep depression, suffering a blockage to publication. He puts a haunting family past behind him and lets go of the critics' scathing and reductive words to finally write another book, his second and last. Jamal's close relationship with Forrester has served as a coronary bypass for Forrester's main problem, a broken heart, which manifested itself in cancer. Jamal's crisis, which offers a parallel subplot, has lain in determining his life's path as a black adolescent.

Forrester notes the underlying existential question present in Jamal's writing: 'What am I going to do with the rest of my life?' When I returned to school later in life to go through the teaching certification program for a second time, I noticed that I now thought much differently about teaching. It wasn't so much about the content anymore; it was about developing other people to their fullest potential. That is what Forrester did with Jamal. I noticed that the movie never gets into the actual novel *Avalon Landing*; instead, it focuses on the relationship between Jamal and Forrester. Watching *Finding Forrester* solidified a lot of ideas I had about writing and the teaching of writing, and it will definitely affect my work with students when I get a job. For example, I myself write expansively and take risks, and I will encourage that in others. And I know that writing is the most multicultural vehicle we humans have for expressing what makes us all different and what makes us all the same. A person's heart is the seat of his/her emotions, identity, and soul. *Finding Forrester* suggests that the quickest way to a person or student's heart can be through his/her writing."

—Heather Beck

⑩

FOSTERING BRILLIANCE

Greg K. Szulgit

USING THESE EXERCISES TO FOSTER BRILLIANCE

What does it take for a student to be brilliant? Certainly, it entails a healthy dose of intelligence, but I think there also has to be an aspect of illumination mixed with it. Students need to take their "book smarts" and electrify them with creativity and imagination. Memorizing the Periodic Table of chemical elements is a neat parlor trick that requires quite a bit of brainpower, but it's the brilliant student who will think of a new way to organize the elements in that table. Playing a piece of music flawlessly requires talent and discipline, but the performance will not be brilliant until the student makes the music speak in a new voice via his or her own interpretation. Intelligence is impressive, but brilliance is inspiring.

The exercises in my other chapters of this book (8, 13, 21, and 34) are not meant to replace curricula. Nor are they meant to focus on "right" and "wrong" answers (although some answers will obviously be more appropriate than others). Instead, these exercises are meant to help the student unlock creative potentials and combine them with intellectual rigor. Sometimes the instructions for these exercises are intentionally vague, allowing the student to "take off" in whatever direction most inspires him or her. At other times, the directions are more specific, but

By: Katie White

don't let that get in the way, please! Remember that the goal is to inspire students to blend their creativity and intellectual prowess. If they come up with their own way to do the assignment, then feel free to readjust the original assignment, or to throw it away altogether and go with the new one. The student will usually produce a much better final product when he or she feels the pride of "owning" the assignment. (In all of my courses, I give students the option of doing extra-credit work. The only criterion, initially, is that they must do a biology-related project that truly interests and inspires them: e.g., critique a science-fiction film, conduct an original experiment, or interview a scientist. Once they have the basic foundation of "their" idea, I set the grading standards for the assignment and I usually set them quite high. Years after the course has ended, they often say that those assignments were some of the most influential on their thinking.)

I have tried to write these exercises so that they can be printed and given to students, who should be able to follow the instructions with minimal guidance. In that sense, the assignments will grant a teacher more freedom with their time, because they can meet with the students at convenient checkpoints. This does not, however, abdicate the teacher from his or her responsibility to spend time with those students. As bright as they may be, they still benefit from a teacher's guidance in helping them reach higher levels of thinking. Keep in touch with them, and let them inspire you.

●

FOUR POPULAR QUESTIONS WITH COMMONSENSE SOLUTIONS

FROM A PARENT

Q: What's the best way to advocate for my gifted child, ensuring she gets the best possible education in her school?

A: YOU are your child's #1 advocate! Your rights as a parent of a gifted child are the same as those of all other parents.

- You have the right to be your child's #1 advocate.
- You have the right to a fair and equitable education for your child.
- You have the right to know when local standardized tests are being given and see sample tests with question and answers.
- You have the right to join your local and state PTA and advocate for the understanding, training, and support of gifted children with programming for the gifted.
- As a member of your school and district PTA, you have the right to expect those organizations to schedule speakers who are experts in the field of gifted education.
- You have the right to know all of your child's test scores and what they mean.
- You have the right to attend study sessions where differentiated curriculums and classrooms with compacted curriculums are explained to you.

- You have the right to expect your child's teacher to love, respect, and educate your child with the same amount of time and dedication she or he gives to all the other children in the classroom.
- You have the right to feel comfortable and supported by the educational system as a parent and advocate for your child, gifted children, and all children.

Know that as you work in school groups, community organizations, and/or neighborhood activities, there will most likely be a prejudice against the gifted. Throughout my career, I even found this attitude in many of my fellow educators and administrators. Terms such as "elitist" or "egotistical" are often levied in arguments against providing appropriate programs and activities for identified gifted children. Unfortunately, this is often due to a lack of understanding of who and what we mean by the term "gifted." Many teachers are still not being educated in differentiating and compacting curriculums, which works for all kids—not just the gifted.

Consequently, it's important for you, the parent, to do your "homework" and familiarize yourself with the definitions and appropriate programming models and curriculum options.

Stay positive as you help other parents and teachers understand this often misunderstood field. Write your local, state, and national political leaders requesting their help in allocating funds and resources for the gifted.

Join your local and state advocacy groups. On the national level, the National Association for Gifted Children (NAGC) provides conferences, publications, and current research about education for the gifted.

One of my favorite stories that I use in advocacy training, reflecting an educational environment and value system in support (or not) of programming in a school district for gifted children, is the *Palcuzzi ploy* (Gallagher and Gallagher 1994, 91–92).

The Palcuzzi Ploy

Mr. Palcuzzi, principal of the Jefferson Elementary School, got tired of hearing objections to special provisions for gifted children, so he decided to spice up an otherwise mild PTA meeting with *his* proposal for gifted children.

The elements of the Palcuzzi program were as follows:

1. Children should be grouped by ability.
2. Part of the school day should be given over to special instruction.
3. Talented students should be allowed time to share their talents with children of other schools in the area or even of other schools throughout the state. (We will pay the transportation costs.)
4. Children should be advanced according to their talents, rather than their age.
5. These children should have specially trained and highly salaried teachers.

As might be expected, the Palcuzzi program was subjected to a barrage of criticism:

"What about the youngsters who aren't able to fit into the special group: won't their egos be damaged?"

"How about the special cost; how could you justify transportation costs that would have to be paid by moving a special group of students from one school to another?"

"Won't we be endangering the children by having them interact with others who are much more mature?"

"Wouldn't the other teachers complain if we gave more money to the instructors of this group?"

After listening for 10 or 15 minutes, Palcuzzi dropped his bomb. He said that he was not describing a *new* program for the intellectually gifted, but a program the school system had been enthusiastically supporting for a number of years—the program for *gifted basketball players*! Palcuzzi took advantage of the silence that followed to review his program again. Ironic, isn't it?

FROM A TEACHER

Q: How do I know if I am truly giving my gifted students the best education they deserve? With the additional burdens of an inclusion classroom, I basically am trying to survive every day. How can I get help and how can I get appropriate training?

A: These are very legitimate questions. Don't despair. Help is available. Staff development training will get you started with understanding who the gifted are and what their academic and emotional needs are, along with differentiating and compacting your curriculum. I have always told parents they have unlimited power and have advised them on how to use it positively, cooperatively, and proactively within their districts and state.

As an educator, you have quite a bit of power, too, by requesting staff development training through your district's teacher center and/or staff development funding. Title I and Jacob Javits grants through local universities can be another source for collaborative funds and training. Start with a staff development coordinator, requesting training, and knowing that what works for gifted children works for all children.

If you want some ideas for training programs, go to my website at www.Partners-For-Excellence.com.

You Are Challenging Your Gifted Students If:

- you are pretesting their knowledge base and compacting their curriculum so they are learning at their aptitude and achievement levels
- you are considering the alternatives of enrichment combined with acceleration and grade-level curriculum
- they are spending somewhat equal amounts of time in class learning and completing appropriate assignments as their peers achieving at grade level
- their writing and speaking reflect a higher level thinking order
- the work they are producing is at the higher level of Bloom's Taxonomy—analysis, synthesis, and evaluation

I've known some districts that differentiate their curriculum for the benefit of their gifted students and expect only these children to produce at the application, synthesis, and evaluation levels, while the

other students are not expected to achieve at these levels at all! Here
we should revise our thinking, as I truly believe we should be training
and expecting *all* of our students to produce at these higher levels of
thinking.

You Know You Are Not Challenging Your Gifted Students If:

- you are having them help the slower achieving students in the
  classroom on a regular or daily basis
- you are having them do grade-level work and they almost always
  finish first or before most of their classmates
- you are giving them "enrichment" activities that are always at
  grade-level expectations
- you are giving them material in which they always get straight As in
  achievement because they already know it
- their writing and speaking reflect "rote memorization"
- the work they are producing is at the lower level of thinking on
  Bloom's Taxonomy—knowledge, comprehension, and application

FROM AN ADMINISTRATOR

Q: Who are the best candidates to hire for teaching the gifted?

A: We are starting to make some progress in requiring teacher candidates to have at least one course of study dealing with gifted children and one course of study in education. A huge problem that ex-
ists is that many undergraduate and graduate colleges still do not
offer such courses.

If a local college does offer such a course I hope all your teacher candidates have taken it, as we know what works for the gifted works for all.
If a course isn't available, the candidates should still be familiar and have
read the outstanding books of Delisle and Galbraith (2001), Winner
(1996), and, of course, Callard-Szulgit (2003a, 2003b).

Check your candidates' knowledge of curriculum compacting, differentiation, and acceleration.

Back in the 1960s and 1970s, principals hired teachers for gifted classes who were popular with the children and parents. One of my colleagues was hired because he was well liked and played the guitar, not to mention being very cute and having all the 5th-grade girls swooning! After two months he resigned and went back to his regular-education assignment. He found out very quickly that he needed understanding, experience, and successful techniques for educating gifted children.

As an administrator, take advantage of staff development programs through your local BOCES. Find out if your area colleges have access to the Jacob Javits monies for gifted education. Send as many teachers as you can for training.

Also feel free to e-mail me at szulgit2@aol.com and check out my website at www.Partners-For-Excellence.com for ideas and staff development programs.

FROM A STUDENT

Q: Why do you say I'm gifted? I'm just like all my friends and really feel funny being labeled.

A: Being gifted academically means that you are achieving or have the potential to achieve at rather high levels when compared with other students of your age and/or grade level. It would be a sad waste of your school days to be studying curriculum you already know or spending a lot of your time tutoring your classmates, wouldn't you agree?

The word *gifted* does often prove to be controversial, causing anxiety such as yours and misunderstandings in others. There are a great many (negative) myths surrounding the entire field of gifted children and education.

While several types of educational programs have proven to positively serve gifted children academically, we do know that what works for the gifted works for all. I fully support an inclusive process rather than an exclusive program. With curriculum differentiation and compacting, all students in a classroom can be educated at their appropriate instructional levels.

You may well be just like all your friends, who might also be academically gifted. If not, I'm sure you all possess the important human gifts of caring, supporting, enjoying life, and being a valued family member.

⑫

FUTURE PROBLEM-SOLVING PROGRAM

I first became aware of the Future Problem-Solving Program when I presented Project Success Enrichment at the First U.S.–China Conference on Education in Beijing in 1996. I was immediately intrigued because of its primary goal of challenging students to think. There are four divisions with which students may become involved:

- Future problem-solving program
- Scenario-writing contest
- Primary division
- Community problem-solving division

Divisions cover K–3, grades 4–6, grades 7–9, and grades 10–12. Teams composed of four students follow a process of six steps to create solutions to hypothetical problems of the future.

I have personally watched one of the schools I worked with—as co-ordinator of Gifted K–8—in Webster (N.Y.) Central School District score on the lower percentile its first year of competition, only to go to the state and national competitive levels the second year.

I credit the dedication and volunteer efforts of the parents who worked diligently and lovingly with our students, especially the Kittleberger family. The learning excitement and team cooperation were absolutely astounding throughout the year-long efforts in the Future Problem-Solving competition.

If you don't have easy access to your local or state contact names, please call Sandra Alcock or Chris Funderburg at (800) 333-5888.

I give this program an absolute A+++ rating!

13

HEARING THE SONG WITHOUT RIGHT OR WRONG

Greg K. Szulgit

A FIRST STEP IN CONQUERING THESIS-INTIMIDATION

One of the biggest problems I face with students is getting them to realize that they can come up with their own valid thesis. For some reason, it is a monumental step for them to propose a unique view on a piece of literature. Fundamentally, they all know how to do this, but they are often intimidated by the prospect of creatively constructing their own, valid opinion on a well-known text. Perhaps it's because they are used to having an authority hand them the "right" answer. They often read a text, but delay actually thinking about it until they get to class, where the topics that they are "supposed" to think about are carefully outlined for them. Yuck! The writing becomes so focused on the task of answering a defined question that it loses one of its most important aspects: creativity.

While students are often intimidated by literature, they can easily form opinions about a complex text when it is presented in a medium or genre with which they feel comfortable. The following exercise is designed as a first step toward overcoming "thesis-intimidation" using popular music lyrics.

1. Ask your students to bring the lyrics of a song that they like to class. Tell them that it helps greatly if the song lyrics are vague in their meaning. They enjoy this because it allows them to feel more involved when they can use their favorite music as a text for a class. Often, they can simply bring in a compact disc jacket and they do not need to write anything down. As a backup plan, you can have a traditional song on hand, such as *Auld Lang Syne* or *Iko Iko*, versions of which are included below. Beatles' songs such as *I Am the Walrus*, *Come Together*, and *Strawberry Fields* (easily found online) work well for more mature audiences.

2. Choose, by whatever method you would like, one of the songs for the entire class to contemplate and read it out loud (or have the student do so—but check the appropriateness of the lyrics first). Ask each student to write what the song, or one part of the song, is about and why they think so (note: they should not write whether or not they liked the song, only what they think it's about). You will probably need to read it again. The students should write for a few minutes without any discussion.

3. When they have finished, ask several of them to read their ideas out loud. If the song is vague enough, you should hear different interpretations of the same source. Ask several of them to defend their ideas, using the lyrics as evidence (of course, you may need to lead them carefully, as they might be nervous about sharing their opinions aloud).

When a few of them have spoken, point out to them that they have each formulated a thesis, whether they know it or not. They have each created a unique opinion concerning an aspect of a text (a song in this case) that nobody else in the room (or the world) has chosen to consider in the same way. Why? Because each person is an individual, and each person interprets a single source differently—which is wonderful! Diversity of opinions adds richness to a text and keeps it fresh.

Creating a thesis is easy! We create them all the time, whether know it or not. The next step becomes defending that thesis, a goal to tackle in another exercise (see chapter 21).

I have composed some questions that might help students with this exercise, although I encourage them to come up with their own. Note that the questions force the students to come up with ideas that do not have easy "right" or "wrong" answers, but instead require a case to be built:

1. What is the song about?
2. Are there "hidden" meanings in the song?
3. What other artists influenced this songwriter?
4. If the performer did not write this song (very common in popular music), can you figure out who did just by listening to the lyrics?
5. Are any characters in the song based on real people and, if so, might you be able to guess whom?

LYRICS TO TRADITIONAL SONGS

Auld Lang Syne

Should auld acquaintance be forgot,
And never brought to mind?
Should auld acquaintance be forgot,

And days of auld lang syne?
And days of auld lang syne, my dear,
And days of auld lang syne.
Should auld acquaintance be forgot,
And days of auld lang syne?

We twa hae run about the braes
And pu'd the gowans fine.
We've wandered mony a weary foot,
Sin' auld lang syne.
Sin' auld lang syne, my dear,
Sin' auld lang syne,
We've wandered mony a weary foot,
Sin' auld ang syne.

We twa hae sported i' the burn,
From morning sun till dine,
But seas between us braid hae roared
Sin' auld lang syne.
Sin' auld lang syne, my dear,
Sin' auld lang syne.
But seas between us braid hae roared
Sin' auld lang syne.

And ther's a hand, my trusty friend,
And gie's a hand o' thine;
We'll tak' a cup o' kindness yet,
For auld lang syne.
For auld lang syne, my dear,
For auld lang syne,
We'll tak' a cup o' kindness yet,
For auld lang syne.

Iko Iko

Hey now (*hey now*)
Hey now (*hey now*)
Iko iko un day
Jockomo feeno ah na nay
Jockomo feena nay
[*repeated twice*]

My spy dog see your spy dog
Sitting by the Bayou
My spy dog see your spy dog
Gonna set your tail on fire

Indian boy going down town
Iko iko un day
You don't like what the big chief said
Said Jockamo feena nay

My grandma see your grandpa
Sitting by the Bayou
My grandma see your grandpa
Gonna set your flag on fire

My spy boy see your spy boy
Sitting by the Bayou
My spy boy see your spy boy
Gonna fix your chicken wire

14

I AM POEMS

I was not familiar with the *I Am* poems until a recent graduate student of mine used them for her creativity project in EDI 648, "Teaching Writing, K–12." The following semester I introduced the format as one of 20 creative writing lessons. The graduate students produced beautiful, personal poems. I asked small groups to read and write responses on the back of each of their classmates' poems. The activity was a huge success and helped the teachers better understand the humanness and writing talents in all of us.

I Am
by Courtney Holzschuh

I am a teacher
I wonder why I can't make them all love to learn
I hear the negativity associated with education
I see how knowledge is taken for granted
I want to show them the gift it can be when embraced
I am a teacher
I pretend that I can reach every student every day
I feel helplessness and sorrow when I realize the truth: they must
    choose to open their minds before they will learn
I touch as many students as I can to make a difference

I worry about the ones beyond my reach
I cry for the future of those afflicted with apathy
I am a teacher
I understand that I cannot save the world
I say that won't make me stop trying
I dream of a day when education is truly valued
I try to instill a thirst for knowledge
I hope my own love for learning is contagious
I am a teacher

I Am
by Bonnie Marciszewski

I wonder if my lessons truly touch the hearts of my students.
I hear both the musical notes of children's laughter and the heart-wrenching sorrow of tears.
I see both smiles and faces darkened by pains I have never known in my lifetime.
I am a teacher and I am a guide.
I want to make school a fun, safe place for all.
I am a teacher and I am a guide.

I pretend that school will offer opening arms of success to each of the children I work with.
I feel agony at the truth to which my imagination tries to betray.
I touch the fiery tips of hope, faith, and childhood dreams.
I worry that on my watch someone will "slip through the cracks."
I cry when youth is denied, and children must grow up too quickly.
I am a teacher and I am a guide.

I understand that I am only one person.
I say anyone can accomplish what they set their hearts and minds to.
I dream that each of my kids will find the "gold" at the rainbow's end.
I try to keep my own youthful flame burning bright.
I hope that I inspire others to greatness.
I am a teacher and I am a guide.

I Am
by Julie Taggart

I am
I am a mother and a worrier.
I wonder if my daughter will grow to be passionate and forgiving.

I hear the clock ticking as time fades.
I see a girl with blonde pigtails and sparkling blue eyes.
I want this girl to be vivacious and happy.

I pretend that we are talking about books and school.
I feel her hand pulling away so she can see the world.
I touch her on the shoulder but she runs away.
I worry that she won't stop to smell the roses.
I cry to know that one day she won't let me in or want me to comfort her.
I am a mother and a worrier.

I understand that she is independent.
I say she can do anything.
I dream about what she will be and inherit.
I try to let her know the enormously satisfying influence she has on me.
I hope one day she will continue the circle.
I am a mother and a worrier.

I Am
by Katie White

I Am a Glistening Mountain Stream . . .
I am a glistening mountain stream
I wonder what treasures are concealed within my depths
I hear children laughing as I tickle their feet
I see deer lapping peacefully at my shores
I want to remain in this serenity forever
I am a glistening mountain stream

I pretend I am flying as I plummet over a waterfall
I feel courageous as I maneuver through jolting rapids
I touch all forms of life with my gentle hands, yet
I worry that I will be taken for granted
I cry thinking of my stagnant body in the dead of summer, until again
I am a glistening mountain stream

I understand how people admire my tranquil splendor
I say, "the world is a beautiful place, take in all it has to offer"
I dream with my eyes open, immersed in this picturesque scenery
I try to provide for each living thing I pass by
I hope this journey will continue on forever
I am a glistening mountain stream

(15)

THE INTERNATIONAL BACCALAUREATE (IB) DIPLOMA PROGRAM

While I have not worked as an educator with the International Baccalaureate (IB) Diploma Program, I have had dozens of graduate students (high school teachers) who have, and they've all raved about this rigorous, preuniversity course of study for highly motivated secondary students.

All IB candidates are required to engage in the study of languages, sciences, mathematics, and humanities in the final two years of their secondary schooling. The IB is designed as a comprehensive curriculum that allows its graduates to fulfill requirements of various national systems of education.

The IB system offers three programs:

- Diploma Program for students in the final two years of school before university, mentioned above
- Middle Years Program for students aged 11 to 16
- Primary Years Program for students aged 3 to 12

The International Baccalaureate Organization provides IB schools around the world with five outstanding services:

- Detailed curriculum guidelines for each program and subject area
- Teacher training workshops

- Online access to 3,000 education resources, subject area experts, and discussion sessions with teachers at IB schools throughout the world
- External assessment of Diploma Program students' work
- Procedures for school-based (internal) assessment of student work

ACADEMIC ADVANTAGES FOR THE SECONDARY INTERNATIONAL BACCALAUREATE COURSE

1. IB courses are college-level courses taught within high school with increased loads of reading and oral/written reports.
2. The final exams are written and evaluated by a panel of professors around the world who are experts in their respective fields.

3. Courses involve an internal assessment, requiring teachers to submit essays and student tapes for grading to external examiners, and/or require visiting examiners to conduct an oral evaluation as part of the assessment procedure.
4. The above assessment helps provide feedback to the classroom teacher and the school administration about the validity and reliability of each class.
5. Final grades are based on more than the results of the final exams as with advanced placement courses. The grading scheme is 1–7, 1 being very poor and 7 being excellent.
6. Many colleges accept higher IB grades as indications of college work well done before a student attends the university. Many seniors are granted waivers for up to one year of college study upon entering the university.

For greater detail of information, go to the IB website: http://web3.ibo .org/ibo/index.cfm/en/ibo/about.

16

LET'S GET REAL: NATIONAL ACADEMIC COMPETITION

Let's Get Real (www.LGReal.org) is a wonderful academic competition providing all participating students an opportunity to work in teams and gain experience with real business challenges. Corporate sponsors supply real challenges for which teams submit solutions in business format. Each team chooses from a list of challenges the one it finds most interesting, including areas such as environmental issues, manufacturing, distribution, software creation, human resources, chemistry, health and safety, facilities design, public relations, engineering, and other areas deemed important to the corporations involved.

Let's Get Real is a 501(c)(3) not-for-profit corporation. There is no entry fee for students or schools. How can you lose? This academic competition provides today's students with the opportunity of choices, application of interests, teamwork, real-world applications, creativity, problem-solving skills, and who knows, maybe even future job employment or a positive connection with a corporation whose challenge was selected for competition.

Parts of this chapter are taken from the Let's Get Real—National Academic Competition website and are used with permission. The website is www.LGReal.org.

RULES AND REGISTRATION

Introduction

Let's Get Real is a competition that gives young students the opportunity to solve real-life issues faced by the sponsoring corporations and provides corporate sponsors with the opportunity to meet talented students. For questions or comments, contact your state coordinator or program coordinator.

Team Eligibility

All 6th- through 12th-grade students from any school are eligible. Students do not have to be affiliated with a school setting to participate . . . in other words, home-schooled children, Boy or Girl Scouts, neighborhood friends, etc., can form teams with an adult coordinator. Students may work on any of the problems. All entries *must* be by teams. *No* individual entries will be considered. Teams must be no smaller than two and no larger than six students. Members of the team may be from the same or different grade levels and may be from the same or different schools. Each team must have at least one adult coordinator.

Adult Coordinator

The team's adult coordinator must be at least 21 years old, be able to provide guidance and direction to the students, and serve as the primary contact with Let's Get Real. A coordinator may sponsor more than one team.

Registration and Contract Forms

Each team must submit a separate *registration form* and *contract form*. Each team may work on more than one problem. However, a separate registration form should be submitted for each problem. The contract form may be duplicated so each team member can submit a separate form for convenience. In addition, a student may be a member of more than one team.

Solving the Problems

The solution must be developed by the students. Parents, teachers, adult coordinators, and other nonteam members may provide training, guidance, transportation, and other indirect assistance only.

Select one or more problems from the sponsors' problem list. Submit a separate registration form and contract form for each problem and for each team. Each entry will be initially judged based on the team's written report. The written report must meet the following requirements (refer also to The Judging Process to see exactly what will be evaluated):

- All assumptions made in arriving at the solution must be clearly stated.
- The costs and benefits of the suggested solution must be clearly stated.
- The written report must be typed and must not exceed 10 double-spaced pages (using 12-point type and 1-inch margins).

- Document all the resources used in arriving at your solution. This includes the time (hours) and money spent. This documentation of expenses is not for reimbursement, but it will be considered in determining the cost-effectiveness of your work as it relates to the quality of your solution.
- Diagrams, drawings, or illustrations and computer simulations or models are acceptable as appendixes to the written report and will not be counted in the page limit. In addition, you may prepare audio- or videotapes, models, or other material helpful to understanding the written report (this material will *not* be returned unless the team is selected for the final oral presentation). However, please note that only finalists selected on the basis of the initial submission will be given an opportunity to make an oral presentation. Therefore, material that requires an accompanying presentation (e.g., 35-mm slides) should be prepared only if the team is invited for an oral presentation.

Submitting Solutions

Please send *all* completed registration forms, contract forms, and solutions by or before the deadline for the specific challenge to:

Let's Get Real
624 Waltonville Road
Hummelstown, PA 17036

The Judging Process

Judging will be done by a panel of employees from the corporate sponsor. Each coprorate sponsor will judge solutions to its own problems usuing the following scoring sheet (rubric developed by Myron E. Yoder, M.Ed., social studies curriculum coordinator at Allentown School District and adjunct professor or education at Cedar Crest College). The written solutions will be judged according to the following criteria:

Practicality or Implementation Potential (10 points). The solution is practical and could be implemented with existing technology.

Effectiveness of the Solution (20 points). The written report is clear, concise, and "sells" the idea. Also, the report meets the style guidelines, is neat and well documented, and is easy to follow.

Cost and Benefit of the Solution (20 points). The cost of the solution is clearly documented, and the benefit of the solution is clearly documented and stated. Also, the analysis of the cost/benefit of the solution is reasonable and understandable.

Creativity and Originality (20 points). The solution is creative and demonstrates thinking beyond the conventional and obvious. The solution also demonstrates ideas developed solely by the group.

Development of the Idea (10 points). There is a chronological log discussion about how your idea was formed, developed, and finally acted on by your group. You may use a narrative in place of a log.

Documentation of the Development of the Solution (20 points). All work and expenses must be clearly documented and appended to the end of the written report. The documentation must be clearly presented and easily understood, and it must be presented in an organized and neat fashion.

Oral Presentations

Finalists will be invited *at their own expense* to the appropriate corporate sponsor's location for an oral presentation. Finalists will be questioned by the judges to determine originality of the idea, knowledge of the subject, and ability to communicate and sell the idea clearly and succinctly. The oral presentation should be limited to 15 minutes, followed by about 10 minutes of questioning by the judges. If your team is invited to the finals, please feel free to employ a PowerPoint presention.

17

LITTLE MAN TATE

The central theme in the movie *Little Man Tate* is the challenge of balancing a gifted child's emotional and intellectual needs and the role of both the parents and the teachers in that effort.

Jodie Foster, a well-known former gifted child herself, directs and stars in *Little Man Tate*, a film about a globally gifted child named Fred Tate. The overriding theme of the movie is that parents and educators must strive together for the healthy social, emotional, and academic success of the whole child, nurturing the special endowments that are present in gifted children, while simultaneously not expecting them to be "little men or women."

Like many individuals with exceptionalities, Fred struggles to find his place in the world. His mom (DeeDee), played by Jodie Foster, does not relate to Fred's giftedness but always supports him emotionally. Jane, a gifted educator from the Grierson Institute, wants to support Fred's intellectual gifts. Jane makes a very powerful point when she states that intelligence is not a disease.

In some ways, Foster's *Little Man Tate* perpetuates many of the myths people already believe in general concerning gifted children and their education: the brilliant educator (Jane), who is sadly lacking in the affect arena; the brash, vulgar, and arrogant Damon, who hides behind a mask of an ignorant mule; and the mother (DeeDee), who is not gifted herself and so does not initially expose her son to academic challenges. All in all, *Little Man Tate* is an intriguing example of the hardships that gifted children face socially and emotionally, not to mention their need for being taught at their academic intellectual level.

I have used this movie in my graduate course "Teaching the Gifted" for several years with great success. It provides a superb forum for discussion and better understanding of gifted children and their relationships with adults—their parents, teachers, peers, and colleagues.

I recommend *Little Man Tate* highly for use in diversity classes, undergraduate and graduate education, psychology courses, parenting classes, and district staff development offerings. Following are some of my graduate students' reactions to *Little Man Tate*.

> "I was pleasantly surprised by the honesty and emotional intensity that came through in the movie *Little Man Tate*, showing just how important it is to be aware of the delicacy of a young gifted mind."
> —Arica Mann

> "I thought it was fascinating to see all of the myths and information that we have mislearned about gifted and talented kids in the movie."
> —Andrea Moore

> "All in all, I loved the movie. My heart really went out to this boy, not because he was neglected by an adult, or by society, but because I truly came to feel that he was alone in spite of the adults that surrounded him!"
> —Alicia Convery

> "Film Rating ★★★★★"
> —Jennifer Warren

> "*Little Man Tate* was truly an insightful and thought-provoking movie. It shines valuable light on the needs of gifted children and their unique characteristics."
> —Rachel Hollenbrand

18

LUNCH BUNCH

To encourage extended math skills in one of the elementary schools I was in charge of as K–8 Coordinator for Gifted in the Webster (N.Y.) Central School District, I asked the 4th-, 5th-, and 6th-grade teachers if they had a group of mathematically gifted children who might want to meet with me once a week to work on challenging math problems. The 4th-grade teachers were thrilled with my offer and opened up the opportunity to any students who might be interested.

We wound up with eight children and met from 12:05 to 12:35 p.m. every Thursday. I pulled the math questions from the current *Math Olympiad* book, placing on the blackboard two 1-minute questions and one 4-minute question to start. Students could work together or individually, however they felt most comfortable. The level of discussions and analytical thinking that went on each lunch period made my heart beat faster with joy.

This was such a nice time together and a wonderful way to teach math skills and problem solving to interested students who already were functioning well above grade level.

In another school, our "lunch bunch" contained 10 4th-, 5th-, and 6th-graders who were reading well beyond their grade-level peers. Again, the opportunity was extended to all.

As an educator, I've always believed that with the greatest "affect" we obtain the greatest cognitive results from our students—all students. Lunch bunch achieved both!

19

MATH QUESTION OF THE DAY, OR "MQ OF D"

I loved doing a Math Question of the Day (MQ of D) with my students, regardless of the grade level and age I taught. It was a great way to expose the children to approximately 120 extra math learnings each year, aside from the specific curriculum we were working on.

The students kept a separate MQ of D notebook just for this purpose. Every morning I placed a new math question on the front board, which the students had to write in their notebooks. They could solve them alone, with a partner, or in groups. The only requirement was that the math problem needed to be solved by lunchtime. The children could bring their notebooks up for the Callard-Szulgit Star of Excellence. Parents were also encouraged to review the math concept we covered that day and provide additional examples for their children at home.

If the math concept was completely new for the students, such as an algebra, geometry, or trigonometry problem, I would teach the concept early in the morning and do one or two math problems with the entire class.

I took the questions from Steven Conrad and Daniel Flegler's *Math Contests*, volumes 1, 2, and 3 at the elementary, middle, and high school levels. Here's an example: A *prime number* is a number greater that 1 whose only whole number factors are itself and 1. What is the smallest prime number greater than 50? Possible answers are: a) 51, b) 52, c) 53, and d) 59.

I also encouraged my students and parents to buy these books and study the types of questions in them.

I was never surprised when my students achieved the highest math scores in the school. This is one more great way to help kids learn, enjoy, and achieve.

20

MINDBENDERS

Most of the intellectually gifted children I've worked with loved to solve puzzles, mindbenders, or any other questions that required a challenge and/or a different style of thinking. The few children who weren't interested were usually perfectionists and fearful of making a mistake. They didn't want to deviate from their very safe routines. Making a mistake or not finding the right answers was unacceptable to them. The gifted perfectionist child is another entire topic, however, and can be studied in my second book, *Perfectionism and Gifted Children* (2003b).

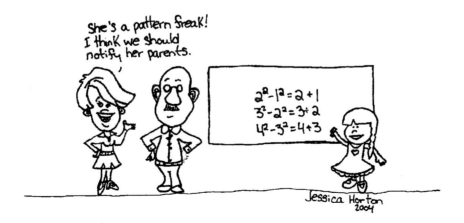

Allen, Skitt, and Gale (1994, 6) state that most people are content to go through life with their brain ticking over at a mere fraction of its true capacity. The intention of their *Mighty Mindbenders* is to present a mind workout that will "bend, stretch, and squeeze your mental powers to the very limit."

This book is filled with more than 200 pages of mind-boggling puzzles, brain teasers, and mazes.

I encourage you to expose your students and your own children to the variety of thinking skills and problem-solving puzzles in *Mindbenders*. Doing these activities together and in a nonthreatening intellectual environment can only excite and enhance, bend, stretch, and squeeze our children's mental powers in a stronger direction.

21

MODIFYING A THESIS:
WATCHING ONE IDEA EVOLVE
INTO SOMETHING ELSE

Greg K. Szulgit

In a previous exercise, Hearing the Song without Right or Wrong (chapter 13), each student practiced creating a thesis. The next step, which is often a frustrating one for them, is to question the validity of their own thesis. It is of utmost importance at this stage that the students see this step as a healthy way to improve their idea by causing it to evolve into something even more interesting than the original one. If they wrap their ego around their original idea, then this step can become adversarial and will only cause them to be further intimidated in the future. I recommend that the teacher first use his or her own thesis as an example and ask the students to assist in its "evolution." If the teacher gracefully accepts change to his or her original idea, then the students should feel less threatened.

The first thing that the students should do is to write down an idea. Then they can begin to ask themselves questions that will help them to modify their original premise. Examples of questions are listed below:

1. Who wrote the song? What about the songwriter's culture, life, time period, etc., might have caused him or her to write those particular words? How is your background different and how might that be influencing your interpretation of the song?

2. What alternative explanations can you come up with for the lyrics? Try to come up with at least four alternatives.

3. How do other parts of the song relate to your idea? Do they support your idea? Does it matter if they do? Does it matter if they do not?

4. On what evidence are you basing your idea? Is there a lot of evidence or a little? If you had to bet money that your idea is right, how much would you be willing to bet?

5. What evidence would you need to increase your confidence in your thesis? How could you obtain this evidence?

Of course, the last question leads into the next step: doing research to further investigate their thesis.

22

NATIONAL GEOGRAPHIC BEE

The National Geographic Bee is a nationwide contest for students in grades 4–8 and is one way to motivate children to learn more about geography. The program is free. Awards are given to individual winners and their participating schools. Winners of state competitions compete in Washington, DC, and the first-place winner at the national level receives a $25,000 college scholarship.

The National Geographic Bee occurs in three stages, beginning at the school level. Schools that register for the bee receive materials to hold competitions. Each school winner takes a written test, with the top 100 scorers in each state and territory competing at the state level. State-level bees are held in the spring. The winner of each state geography bee proceeds to the national competition. The 55 state and territory winners meet at National Geographic Society Headquarters in Washington, DC, for the final competition, where the number of contestants is narrowed to 10 finalists, each competing for the first-place prize of a $25,000 college scholarship. The second- and third-place winners receive $15,000 and $10,000 scholarships, respectively. *Jeopardy!* host Alex Trebek moderates the final competition.

Principals with students in grades 4–8 must register their schools to participate in the National Geographic Bee before the October 15 deadline. Principals may register by writing on school letterhead and enclosing a $40 check made payable to the National Geographic Society at the following address. Materials for the school bees are mailed to registered schools in November. For more information, write to The National Geographic Bee, National Geographic Society, 1145 17th St., NW, Washington, DC, 20036-4688, or visit www.nationalgeographic.com/geographybee/basics.html.

(23)

NEWBERY AND CALDECOTT AWARD–WINNING BOOKS

THE NEWBERY AWARD

The Newbery Award for original and creative work in the field of children's books was first awarded in 1922 to Hendrik Willem van Loon for *The Story of Mankind*. Since its inception, more than 80 award-winning books have received the prestigious John Newbery Medal and well over 200 additional books have received honors.

My personal all-time Newbery favorite is Robert C. O'Brien's *Mrs. Frisby and the Rats of NIMH*, followed by Spinelli's *Maniac Magee*, Paterson's *Bridge to Terabithia*, and Raskin's *The Westing Game*. I've read all the Newberys.

I still remember sitting up in bed exclaiming, "No, please, no!" when Leslie accidentally died in *Terabithia*. I read *Mrs. Frisby* to my classes every year, whether teaching middle, intermediate, or primary school children, and the students love it.

The Newbery books present dilemmas, problem solving, life experiences, family support, and interactions with enriched vocabulary, ad infinitum. I've yet to meet a gifted student who wasn't intrigued and delighted with the Newbery books.

While I was teaching a self-contained 4th-grade class of gifted students (many years ago), I developed a Newbery Club to accelerate reading of fine literature in my classroom. I applied to our school's PTA for a $300 grant to get started and received it. With parent volunteers, we began by modeling a Newbery membership card after our school's computer club membership card. We made 25 buttons with our school's button machine, using a picture of the Newbery bronze medal designed by René Paul Chambellan back in 1921.

Great news! Within two years, the Newbery Club became a schoolwide incentive reading program for our 4th, 5th, and 6th grades, sponsored by the profits from the library's yearly book fair. We also had 3rd-graders reading Newberys, as well as five gifted 2nd-graders. In fact, one of the 3rd-graders broke all the school records initially established and received all the prizes we had to offer by the end of 4th grade. We reworked the award system and extended the top award to the reading of 150 Newbery books and prizes that could be cumulative throughout the child's schooling. The Newbery Club became a wonderful, schoolwide, outstanding reading incentive.

I have included a copy of our original Newbery Club Award Sheet and an overview of the John Newbery Award, as well as the following list of award-winning books. Happy reading and awarding!

Newbery Medal Winners, 1922–2004

- 2004: *The Tale of Despereaux: Being the Story of a Mouse, a Princess, Some Soup, and a Spool of Thread* by Kate DiCamillo (Candlewick Press)
- 2003: *Crispin: The Cross of Lead* by Avi (Hyperion)
- 2002: *A Single Shard* by Linda Sue Park (Houghton Mifflin)
- 2001: *A Year Down Yonder* by Richard Peck (Dial)
- 2000: *Bud, Not Buddy* by Christopher Paul Curtis (Delacorte)
- 1999: *Holes* by Louis Sachar (Frances Foster)
- 1998: *Out of the Dust* by Karen Hesse (Scholastic)
- 1997: *The View from Saturday* by E. L. Konigsburg (Jean Karl/Atheneum)
- 1996: *The Midwife's Apprentice* by Karen Cushman (Clarion)
- 1995: *Walk Two Moons* by Sharon Creech (HarperCollins)
- 1994: *The Giver* by Lois Lowry (Houghton)
- 1993: *Missing May* by Cynthia Rylant (Jackson/Orchard)
- 1992: *Shiloh* by Phyllis Reynolds Naylor (Atheneum)

- 1991: *Maniac Magee* by Jerry Spinelli (Little, Brown)
- 1990: *Number the Stars* by Lois Lowry (Houghton)
- 1989: *Joyful Noise: Poems for Two Voices* by Paul Fleischman (Harper)
- 1988: *Lincoln: A Photobiography* by Russell Freedman (Clarion)
- 1987: *The Whipping Boy* by Sid Fleischman (Greenwillow)
- 1986: *Sarah, Plain and Tall* by Patricia MacLachlan (Harper)
- 1985: *The Hero and the Crown* by Robin McKinley (Greenwillow)
- 1984: *Dear Mr. Henshaw* by Beverly Cleary (Morrow)
- 1983: *Dicey's Song* by Cynthia Voigt (Atheneum)
- 1982: *A Visit to William Blake's Inn: Poems for Innocent and Experienced Travelers* by Nancy Willard (Harcourt)
- 1981: *Jacob Have I Loved* by Katherine Paterson (Crowell)
- 1980: *A Gathering of Days: A New England Girl's Journal, 1830–1832* by Joan W. Blos (Scribner)
- 1979: *The Westing Game* by Ellen Raskin (Dutton)
- 1978: *Bridge to Terabithia* by Katherine Paterson (Crowell)
- 1977: *Roll of Thunder, Hear My Cry* by Mildred D. Taylor (Dial)
- 1976: *The Grey King* by Susan Cooper (McElderry/Atheneum)
- 1975: *M. C. Higgins, the Great* by Virginia Hamilton (Macmillan)
- 1974: *The Slave Dancer* by Paula Fox (Bradbury)
- 1973: *Julie of the Wolves* by Jean Craighead George (Harper)
- 1972: *Mrs. Frisby and the Rats of NIMH* by Robert C. O'Brien (Atheneum)
- 1971: *Summer of the Swans* by Betsy Byars (Viking)
- 1970: *Sounder* by William H. Armstrong (Harper)
- 1969: *The High King* by Lloyd Alexander (Holt)
- 1968: *From the Mixed-Up Files of Mrs. Basil E. Frankweiler* by E. L. Konigsburg (Atheneum)
- 1967: *Up a Road Slowly* by Irene Hunt (Follett)
- 1966: *I, Juan de Pareja* by Elizabeth Borton de Trevino (Farrar)
- 1965: *Shadow of a Bull* by Maia Wojciechowska (Atheneum)
- 1964: *It's Like This, Cat* by Emily Neville (Harper)
- 1963: *A Wrinkle in Time* by Madeleine L'Engle (Farrar)
- 1962: *The Bronze Bow* by Elizabeth George Speare (Houghton)
- 1961: *Island of the Blue Dolphins* by Scott O'Dell (Houghton)
- 1960: *Onion John* by Joseph Krumgold (Crowell)

- 1959: *The Witch of Blackbird Pond* by Elizabeth George Speare (Houghton)
- 1958: *Rifles for Watie* by Harold Keith (Crowell)
- 1957: *Miracles on Maple Hill* by Virginia Sorenson (Harcourt)
- 1956: *Carry On, Mr. Bowditch* by Jean Lee Latham (Houghton)
- 1955: *The Wheel on the School* by Meindert DeJong (Harper)
- 1954: *. . . And Now Miguel* by Joseph Krumgold (Crowell)
- 1953: *Secret of the Andes* by Ann Nolan Clark (Viking)
- 1952: *Ginger Pye* by Eleanor Estes (Harcourt)
- 1951: *Amos Fortune, Free Man* by Elizabeth Yates (Dutton)
- 1950: *The Door in the Wall* by Marguerite de Angeli (Doubleday)
- 1949: *King of the Wind* by Marguerite Henry (Rand McNally)
- 1948: *The Twenty-One Balloons* by William Pène du Bois (Viking)
- 1947: *Miss Hickory* by Carolyn Sherwin Bailey (Viking)
- 1946: *Strawberry Girl* by Lois Lenski (Lippincott)
- 1945: *Rabbit Hill* by Robert Lawson (Viking)
- 1944: *Johnny Tremain* by Esther Forbes (Houghton)
- 1943: *Adam of the Road* by Elizabeth Janet Gray (Viking)
- 1942: *The Matchlock Gun* by Walter Edmonds (Dodd)
- 1941: *Call It Courage* by Armstrong Sperry (Macmillan)
- 1940: *Daniel Boone* by James Daugherty (Viking)
- 1939: *Thimble Summer* by Elizabeth Enright (Rinehart)
- 1938: *The White Stag* by Kate Seredy (Viking)
- 1937: *Roller Skates* by Ruth Sawyer (Viking)
- 1936: *Caddie Woodlawn* by Carol Ryrie Brink (Macmillan)
- 1935: *Dobry* by Monica Shannon (Viking)
- 1934: *Invincible Louisa: The Story of the Author of "Little Women"* by Cornelia Meigs (Little, Brown)
- 1933: *Young Fu of the Upper Yangtze* by Elizabeth Lewis (Winston)
- 1932: *Waterless Mountain* by Laura Adams Armer (Longmans)
- 1931: *The Cat Who Went to Heaven* by Elizabeth Coatsworth (Macmillan)
- 1930: *Hitty, Her First Hundred Years* by Rachel Field (Macmillan)
- 1929: *The Trumpeter of Krakow* by Eric P. Kelly (Macmillan)
- 1928: *Gay Neck, the Story of a Pigeon* by Dhan Gopal Mukerji (Dutton)
- 1927: *Smoky, the Cowhorse* by Will James (Scribner)

- 1926: *Shen of the Sea* by Arthur Bowie Chrisman (Dutton)
- 1925: *Tales from Silver Lands* by Charles Finger (Doubleday)
- 1924: *The Dark Frigate* by Charles Boardman Hawes (Little, Brown)
- 1923: *The Voyages of Doctor Dolittle* by Hugh Lofting (Lippincott)
- 1922: *The Story of Mankind* by Hendrik Willem van Loon (Liveright)

For further information on the Newbery Medal winners, visit http://www.ala.org/alsc/nquick.html.

THE CALDECOTT AWARD

In conjunction with the John Newbery awards for prestigious children's literature, the first Caldecott Medal was awarded to illustrator Dorothy P. Lathrop for *Animals of the Bible, A Picture Book* in 1938. This award is presented yearly to the artist creating the most distinguished American picture book for children published in the United States. The medal is given in honor of Randolph Caldecott, a nineteenth-century English illustrator.

I have used many of the Caldecott books for my creative-writing lessons over the years, at all grade levels, my favorite being Van Allsburg's *The Polar Express*, 1986. I have also used these beautifully illustrated books with my students whose gifts are in the artistic arena.

While I toyed with starting a Caldecott Club similar to our Newbery Club to award our school's gifted artists, I didn't . . . one of my regrets. However, I hope this chapter spurs one or more of you creative parents and/or art educators reading this book to develop your own Caldecott Clubs for your school. Please let me know if you do. My heart will be happy!

Caldecott Medal Winners, 1938–2004

- 2004: *The Man Who Walked between the Towers* by Mordicai Gerstein (Roaring Brook Press/Millbrook Press)
- 2003: *My Friend Rabbitt* by Eric Rohmann (Roaring Brook Press/Millbrook Press)

- 2002: *The Three Pigs* by David Wiesner (Clarion/Houghton Mifflin)
- 2001: *So You Want to Be President?* illustrated by David Small; text: Judith St. George (Philomel)
- 2000: *Joseph Had a Little Overcoat* by Simms Taback (Viking)
- 1999: *Snowflake Bentley*, illustrated by Mary Azarian; text: Jacqueline Briggs Martin (Houghton)
- 1998: *Rapunzel* by Paul O. Zelinsky (Dutton)
- 1997: *Golem* by David Wisniewski (Clarion)
- 1996: *Officer Buckle and Gloria* by Peggy Rathmann (Putnam)
- 1995: *Smoky Night*, illustrated by David Diaz; text: Eve Bunting (Harcourt)
- 1994: *Grandfather's Journey* by Allen Say; edited by Walter Lorraine (Houghton)
- 1993: *Mirette on the High Wire* by Emily Arnold McCully (Putnam)
- 1992: *Tuesday* by David Wiesner (Clarion)
- 1991: *Black and White* by David Macaulay (Houghton)
- 1990: *Lon Po Po: A Red-Riding Hood Story from China* by Ed Young (Philomel)
- 1989: *Song and Dance Man*, illustrated by Stephen Gammell; text: Karen Ackerman (Knopf)
- 1988: *Owl Moon*, illustrated by John Schoenherr; text: Jane Yolen (Philomel)
- 1987: *Hey, Al*, illustrated by Richard Egielski; text: Arthur Yorinks (Farrar)
- 1986: *The Polar Express* by Chris Van Allsburg (Houghton)
- 1985: *Saint George and the Dragon*, illustrated by Trina Schart Hyman; text: retold by Margaret Hodges (Little, Brown)
- 1984: *The Glorious Flight: Across the Channel with Louis Bleriot* by Alice and Martin Provensen (Viking)
- 1983: *Shadow*, translated and illustrated by Marcia Brown; original text in French: Blaise Cendrars (Scribner)
- 1982: *Jumanji* by Chris Van Allsburg (Houghton)
- 1981: *Fables* by Arnold Lobel (Harper)
- 1980: *Ox-Cart Man*, illustrated by Barbara Cooney; text: Donald Hall (Viking)
- 1979: *The Girl Who Loved Wild Horses* by Paul Goble (Bradbury)

- 1978: *Noah's Ark* by Peter Spier (Doubleday)
- 1977: *Ashanti to Zulu: African Traditions*, illustrated by Leo and Diane Dillon; text: Margaret Musgrove (Dial)
- 1976: *Why Mosquitoes Buzz in People's Ears*, illustrated by Leo and Diane Dillon; text: retold by Verna Aardema (Dial)
- 1975: *Arrow to the Sun* by Gerald McDermott (Viking)
- 1974: *Duffy and the Devil*, illustrated by Margot Zemach; text: retold by Harve Zemach (Farrar)
- 1973: *The Funny Little Woman*, illustrated by Blair Lent; text: retold by Arlene Mosel (Dutton)
- 1972: *One Fine Day* by Nonny Hogrogian (Macmillan)
- 1971: *A Story, a Story* by Gail E. Haley (Atheneum)
- 1970: *Sylvester and the Magic Pebble* by William Steig (Windmill Books)
- 1969: *The Fool of the World and the Flying Ship*, illustrated by Uri Shulevitz; text: retold by Arthur Ransome (Farrar)
- 1968: *Drummer Hoff*, illustrated by Ed Emberley; text: adapted by Barbara Emberley (Prentice-Hall)
- 1967: *Sam, Bangs, and Moonshine* by Evaline Ness (Holt)
- 1966: *Always Room for One More*, illustrated by Nonny Hogrogian; text: Sorche Nic Leodhas, pseud. [Leclair Alger] (Holt)
- 1965: *May I Bring a Friend?* illustrated by Beni Montresor; text: Beatrice Schenk de Regniers (Atheneum)
- 1964: *Where the Wild Things Are* by Maurice Sendak (Harper)
- 1963: *The Snowy Day* by Ezra Jack Keats (Viking)
- 1962: *Once a Mouse* by Marcia Brown (Scribner)
- 1961: *Baboushka and the Three Kings*, illustrated by Nicolas Sidjakov; text: Ruth Robbins (Parnassus)
- 1960: *Nine Days to Christmas*, illustrated by Marie Hall Ets; text: Marie Hall Ets and Aurora Labastida (Viking)
- 1959: *Chanticleer and the Fox*, illustrated by Barbara Cooney; text: adapted from Chaucer's *Canterbury Tales* by Barbara Cooney (Crowell)
- 1958: *Time of Wonder* by Robert McCloskey (Viking)
- 1957: *A Tree Is Nice*, illustrated by Marc Simont; text: Janice Udry (Harper)

- 1956: *Frog Went A-Courtin'*, illustrated by Feodor Rojankovsky; text: retold by John Langstaff (Harcourt)
- 1955: *Cinderella; or, The Little Glass Slipper*, illustrated by Marcia Brown; text: translated from Charles Perrault by Marcia Brown (Scribner)
- 1954: *Madeline's Rescue* by Ludwig Bemelmans (Viking)
- 1953: *The Biggest Bear* by Lynd Ward (Houghton)
- 1952: *Finders Keepers*, illustrated by Nicolas, pseud. [Nicholas Mordvinoff]; text: Will, pseud. [William Lipkind] (Harcourt)
- 1951: *The Egg Tree* by Katherine Milhous (Scribner)
- 1950: *Song of the Swallows* by Leo Politi (Scribner)
- 1949: *The Big Snow* by Berta and Elmer Hader (Macmillan)
- 1948: *White Snow, Bright Snow*, illustrated by Roger Duvoisin; text: Alvin Tresselt (Lothrop)
- 1947: *The Little Island*, illustrated by Leonard Weisgard; text: Golden MacDonald, pseud. [Margaret Wise Brown] (Doubleday)
- 1946: *The Rooster Crows* by Maude and Miska Petersham (Macmillan)
- 1945: *Prayer for a Child*, illustrated by Elizabeth Orton Jones; text: Rachel Field (Macmillan)
- 1944: *Many Moons*, illustrated by Louis Slobodkin; text: James Thurber (Harcourt)
- 1943: *The Little House* by Virginia Lee Burton (Houghton)
- 1942: *Make Way for Ducklings* by Robert McCloskey (Viking)
- 1941: *They Were Strong and Good* by Robert Lawson (Viking)
- 1940: *Abraham Lincoln* by Ingri and Edgar Parin d'Aulaire (Doubleday)
- 1939: *Mei Li* by Thomas Handforth (Doubleday)
- 1938: *Animals of the Bible, A Picture Book*, illustrated by Dorothy P. Lathrop; text: selected by Helen Dean Fish (Lippincott)

You may also access more information about the Caldecotts and Newberys on the Internet at: http://www.ala.org/alsc/cquide.html.

I've started asking my graduate students what their favorite books have been while growing up, and have included their most popular titles in table 23.1 for your children's reading pleasure. Enjoy!

Table 23.1

Favorite Children's Books

Author	Title
Adler, David A.	Young Cam Jansen and the Missing Cookie
Arnold, Tedd	Ollie Forgot
Banks, Lynne Reid	The Indian in the Cupboard
Berenstain, Stan and Jan	Say Please and Thank You
Berenstain, Stan and Jan	All of the Berenstain Bears books
Blume, Judy	Are You There, God? It's Me, Margaret
Blume, Judy	Superfudge
Brittain, Bill	All the Money in the World
Brown, Margaret Wise	Goodnight Moon
Burnford, Sheila	The Incredible Journey
Burton, Virginia Lee	Mike Mulligan and His Steam Shovel
Caswell, Brian	A Cage of Butterflies
Cleary, Beverly	The Mouse and the Motorcycle
Cooney, Caroline B.	What Child Is This?
Cutts, David, and Don Sliverstein	The House That Jack Built
Dahl, Roald	The BFG
Dahl, Roald	Charlie and the Chocolate Factory
Dahl, Roald	James and the Giant Peach
Dr. Seuss	Horton Hears a Who!
Dr. Seuss	The Cat in the Hat
Dr. Seuss	The Lorax
Dr. Seuss	Yertle the Turtle and Other Stories
Eager, Edward	Half Magic
Erdrich, Louise	The Birchbark House
Fitzgerald, John D.	The Great Brain
Fitzhugh, Louise	Harriet the Spy
Fox, Mem	Wilfrid Gordon McDonald Partridge
George, Jean Craighead	Julie of the Wolves
Gramatky, Hardie	Little Toot
Hamilton, Virginia	M. C. Higgins, the Great
Hazel, Beth, and Jerome C. Harste	My Icky Picky Sister
Juster, Norton	The Phantom Tollbooth
Keats, Ezra Jack	The Snowy Day
Konigsburg, E. L.	From the Mixed-Up Files of Mrs. Basil E. Frankweiler
Lehne, Judith Logan	When the Ragman Sings
L'Engle, Madeleine	A Wrinkle in Time
Le Tord, Bijou	A Blue Butterfly: A Story about Claude Monet
Lewis, C. S.	The Lion, the Witch, and the Wardrobe
Littledale, Freya	The Magic Fish
Lobel, Arnold	Frog and Toad Are Friends
Lobel, Arnold	Frog and Toad Together

(continued)

Favorite Children's Books

Author	Title
London, Jack	Call of the Wild
London, Jonathan	Froggy Plays Soccer
Loupy, Christopher	Hugs and Kisses
Mayer, Mercer	Just Grandma and Me
Mendez, Phil	The Black Snowman
Munsch, Robert	Love You Forever
Munsch, Robert	The Paper Bag Princess
Norton, Mary	The Borrowers
O'Brien, Robert C.	Mrs. Frisby and the Rats of NIMH
O'Dell, Scott	Island of the Blue Dolphins
Ottley, Ted	Code of Deception
Paulsen, Gary	Hatchet
Park, Barbara	Junie B. Jones Has a Peep in Her Pocket
Park, Barbara	The Kid in the Red Jacket
Paterson, Katherine	Bridge to Terabithia
Pinkwater, Daniel	Five Novels: Alan Mendelsohn, the Boy from Mars; Slaves of Speigel; The Last Guru; Young Adult Novel; The Snarkout Boys and the Avocado of Death
Pullman, Philip	The Golden Compass
Rawls, Wilson	Where the Red Fern Grows
Rowling, J. K.	Harry Potter and the Goblet of Fire
Rowling, J. K.	Harry Potter and the Sorcerer's Stone
Sachar, Louis	Holes
Saltzman, David	The Jester Has Lost His Jingle
Selden, George	The Cricket in Times Square
Sendak, Maurice	Where the Wild Things Are
Shannon, David	A Bad Case of Stripes
Silverstein, Shel	The Giving Tree
Silverstein, Shel	The Missing Piece
Speare, Elizabeth George	The Witch of Blackbird Pond
Steig, William	Dominic
Taylor, Mildred D.	Roll of Thunder, Hear My Cry
Tolan, Stephanie S.	Welcome to the Ark
Van Allsburg, Chris	The Polar Express
Viorst, Judith	Alexander and the Terrible, Horrible, No Good, Very Bad Day
Waber, Bernard	Ira Sleeps Over
White, E. B.	Charlotte's Web
Wiesner, David	The Three Pigs
Wiesner, David	Tuesday
Williams, Margery	The Velveteen Rabbit

Table 23.1 (continued)

Favorite Books with a Gifted Primary Character

Author	Title
Bambara, Toni Cade	*Raymond's Run*
Bemelmans, Ludwig	*Madeline*
Brighton, Catherine	*The Fossil Girl*
Brown, Margaret Wise	*The Runaway Bunny*
Burnett, Frances Hodgson	*A Little Princess*
Bush, Timothy	*Grunt! The Primitive Cave Boy*
Carmody, Isobelle	*Obernewtyn*
Caswell, Brian	*A Cage of Butterflies*
Chesworth, Michael	*Archibald Frisby*
Cleary, Beverly	*Ramona the Brave*
Clements, Andrew	*The Landry News*
Cohen, Barbara	*213 Valentines*
Cooper, Susan	*The Dark Is Rising*
Dahl, Roald	*Charlie and the Chocolate Factory*
Davidson, Margaret	*Helen Keller* (Scholastic Biography)
Estes, Eleanor	*The Hundred Dresses*
Fleischman, Paul	*Weslandia*
Forbes, Esther	*Johnny Tremain*
Galdone, Paul	*The Little Red Hen*
Hinton, S. E.	*The Outsiders*
Hoffmann, Mary	*Amazing Grace*
Jacques, Brian	*Redwall*
Jones, Diana Wynne	*Charmed Life*
Jones, Diana Wynne	*The Lives of Christopher Chant*
Kallok, Emma	*The Diary of Chickabiddy Baby*
King-Smith, Dick	*A Mouse Called Wolf*
Klein, Robin	*Halfway Across the Galaxy and Turn Left*
Konigsburg, E. L.	*The View from Saturday*
Lackey, Mercedes	*Magic's Pawn*
Le Guin, Ursula K.	The Earthsea trilogy
L'Engel, Madeleine	*A Ring of Endless Light*
Lindgren, Astrid	*Pippi Longstocking*
Lowry, Lois	*Anastasia Krupnik*
Lowry, Lois	*The Giver*
McLerran, Alice	*Roxaboxen*
Montague, Jeanne	*Midnight Moon*
Montgomery, L. M.	*Anne of Green Gables*
Moon, Nicola	*Lucy's Picture*
Myers, Walter Dean	*Darnell Rock Reporting*
Nostlinger, Christine	*Konrad*

(continued)

Table 23.1 (*continued*)

Favorite Books with a Gifted Primary Character

Author	Title
Odgers, Sally	*Translations in Celadon*
Parish, Peggy	*Amelia Bedelia*
Potok, Chaim	*The Chosen*
Rachlin, Ann	*Mozart*
Richter, Conrad	*The Light in the Forest*
Rowling, J. K.	*Harry Potter and the Goblet of Fire*
Rowling, J. K.	*Harry Potter and the Sorcerer's Stone*
Salinger, J. D.	*The Catcher in the Rye*
Scieszka, Jon	*The True Story of the Three Little Pigs*
Spinelli, Jerry	*Maniac Magee*
Stewart, Sarah	*The Gardener*
Tusa, Tricia	*Bunnies in My Head*
Venezia, Mike	*Picasso*
White, E. B.	*Charlotte's Web*
Wilder, Laura Ingalls	*Little Town in the Big Woods*
Williams, Margery	*The Velveteen Rabbit*

Favorite Middle School Books

Author	Title
Adams, Richard	*Watership Down*
Anderson, Laurie Halse	*Speak*
Atwater, Richard, and Florence Atwater	*Mr. Popper's Penguins*
Blume, Judy	*Are You There, God? It's Me, Margaret*
Brashares, Ann	*The Sisterhood of the Traveling Pants*
Collier, James Lincoln, and Christopher Collier	*My Brother Sam Is Dead*
Crutcher, Chris	*Staying Fat for Sarah Byrnes*
Dickens, Charles	*Great Expectations*
Fanon, Frantz	*Black Skin, White Masks*
Fitzgerald, F. Scott	*The Great Gatsby*
Fleischman, Paul	*Whirligig*
Hahn, Mary Downing	*Daphne's Book*
Hinton, S. E.	*The Outsiders*
Hunt, Irene	*Across Five Aprils*
L'Engle, Madeleine	*A Wrinkle in Time*
Lowry, Lois	*Number the Stars*
Paterson, Katherine	*Bridge to Terabithia*
Sachar, Louis	*Holes*
Salinger, J. D.	*The Catcher in the Rye*
Simon, Seymour	*The Heart: Our Circulatory System*
Spinelli, Jerry	*Stargirl*
Tolen, Stephanie S.	*Surviving the Applewhites*

Table 23.1 (*continued*)

Favorite Middle School Books

Author	Title
Wolff, Virginia Euwer	*Bat 6*
Yolen, Jane	*The Devil's Arithmetic*
Zindel, Paul	*The Pigman*

Favorite High School Books

Author	Title
Anderson, Laurie Halse	*Speak*
Atwood, Margaret	*The Handmaid's Tale*
Babbitt, Natalie	*Tuck Everlasting*
Bach, Richard	*Jonathan Livingston Seagull*
Blume, Judy	*Are You There, God? It's Me, Margaret*
Blume, Judy	*Blubber*
Blume, Judy	*Summer Sisters*
Burnford, Sheila	*The Incredible Journey*
Carmichael, Stokely S., and Charles V. Hamilton	*Black Power: The Politics of Liberation in America*
Catling, Patrick Skene	*The Chocolate Touch*
Chopin, Kate	*The Awakening*
Crane, Stephen	*Red Badge of Courage*
DeFelice, Cynthia	*The Ghost of Fossil Glen*
Evans, Nicolas	*The Horse Whisperer*
Fleischman, Paul	*Whirligig*
Haddix, Margaret Peterson	*Among the Hidden*
Hansberry, Lorraine	*A Raisin in the Sun*
Hinton, S. E.	*The Outsiders*
Gaines, Ernest J.	*A Lesson before Dying*
Golding, William	*Lord of the Flies*
Goodrich, Frances	*The Diary of Anne Frank*
James, George G. M.	*Stolen Legacy*
Keene, Carolyn	*The Bungalow Mystery*
King, Stephen	*The Stand*
Konigsburg, E. L.	*From the Mixed-Up Files of Mrs. Basil E. Frankweiler*
Lamb, Wally	*She's Come Undone*
Lee, Harper	*To Kill a Mockingbird*
Lester, Julius	*Othello: A Novel*
Martin, Ann M.	Baby-Sitters Club books
Miller, Arthur	*The Crucible*
Mitchell, Margaret	*Gone with the Wind*
O'Brien, Tim	*The Things They Carried*
Orwell, George	*Animal Farm*
Paterson, Katherine	*Bridge to Terabithia*
Paulsen, Gary	*Hatchet*

(continued)

Table 23.1 (*continued*)

Favorite High School Books

Author	Title
Pelzer, Dave	A Child Called "It": One Child's Courage to Survive
Quarles, Heather	A Door Near Here
Quindlen, Anna	Black and Blue
Rand, Ayn	Atlas Shrugged
Rand, Ayn	The Fountainhead
Rawls, Wilson	Where the Red Fern Grows
Rockwell, Thomas	How to Eat Fried Worms
Ruckman, Ivy	Night of the Twisters
Sachar, Louis	Holes
Salinger, J. D.	The Catcher in the Rye
Shakespeare, William	Othello
Shelley, Mary	Frankenstein
Simon, Neil	Biloxi Blues
Spinelli, Jerry	Maniac Magee
Spinelli, Jerry	Stargirl
Spinelli, Jerry	Wringer
Steinbeck, John	Of Mice and Men
Steinbeck, John	The Pearl
Taylor, Mildred D.	Roll of Thunder, Hear My Cry
Uris, Leon	Exodus
X, Malcolm, with Alex Haley	The Autobiography of Malcolm X
Yolen, Jane	The Devil's Arithmetic
Wiesel, Elie	Night

(24)

PLACE-VALUE GAMES

The information in this chapter is adapted from Jennifer Warren's EDI 651 creativity project entitled "Teaching the Gifted Child."

PROJECT RATIONALE

"Place value" is a math concept that is difficult for some students to grasp as well as demonstrate their understanding of. These games are designed to help students demonstrate their knowledge while working at their own instructional level. The games are differentiated so the students can work to their own level of ability and understanding.

GAME DESCRIPTIONS

High Rollin' Bowlin'!

In High Rollin' Bowlin'!, students bowl to knock down as many numbered pins as desired to make the biggest number possible. If they are working on reading two-digit numbers, they will have only two pins set up and try to knock down only those pins. If they are working on reading and understanding three- or four-digit numbers, they will try to hit that many pins down and order them to make the largest number possible. If students want an extra challenge to demonstrate a full understanding of place value, they can set up all ten pins and order as many as they can knock down to make the biggest number possible. The students in all situations must be able to read the number they made.

Duck Hunt!

In Duck Hunt!, students select a plastic duck from a "pond," read the number on the bottom, and record the number in the place they choose on a sentence strip to make the biggest number they can. If they are working on two-digit numbers, they will select only two ducks to order. If they are working on reading four-digit numbers, they will select four ducks to order. If they are working on six-digit numbers, they will select six ducks from the pond.

Bean-Bag Hop!

In Bean-Bag Hop!, students use a modified Twister® mat and toss bean bags onto the prenumbered circles. They then try to order the numbers they landed on to make the biggest number they can. Again, this is differentiated based on student ability. If students need work on reading two digits, they toss onto only two circles. If they are working on seven digits, they will toss the bean bag seven times.

You Shoot, You Score!

In You Shoot, You Score!, students use a hockey stick and puck to shoot for numbers. There is a scoring area for the students to aim at. In this area, there are the numbers from zero to nine. If they are working on reading and understanding two-digit numbers, they will shoot only twice. If they are working on higher numbers, they will shoot accordingly. The students need to record their scores and then put the numbers in order to make the biggest number they can, and then read the number aloud.

25

THE PRESIDENT'S
FITNESS CHALLENGE

For those of you who read my first two books, you know how much I support physical fitness as an important activity for the mental as well as the physical health of our children. The President's Challenge for Kids is another wonderful way to encourage our children to become involved in activities, meet challenges, earn rewards, and be part of a group.

There are four groups supported in this fitness challenge: Kids, 3–12; Teens, 13–17; Adults, 18–64, and Seniors 65+. Signing up for a group is simple and you win awards for staying active, while tracking your progress along with other kids or adults across America.

As a matter of fact, I became an active member of this challenge while I was writing this book. Happily, I fit into the adult category and signed on for the "active lifestyle." Perhaps a year from now, I'll be up for the Presidential Champions Group.

The President's Fitness Challenge is also an excellent idea as an entire school project. I can easily see a PTA donating funds to support the T-shirt, badge awards, and other prizes for positive and forward-moving behaviors of its students.

For more information, go to http://www.presidentschallenge.org.

26

PROJECT SUCCESS ENRICHMENT: A NATIONALLY RECOGNIZED, EXEMPLARY LANGUAGE ARTS AND WRITING PROGRAM

Throughout my career, I have never been a slouch when it comes to creativity and its many wonderful uses. I also have never been at a loss when it comes to integrating curricular materials. However, when I was first introduced to Project Success Enrichment (PSE) at a 10-state referendum of nationally recognized, exemplary programs in the National Diffusion Network 15 years ago, I was absolutely awed. PSE oozes with creative and powerful integrative lessons for teachers and students. I immediately came back to Rochester, New York, and wrote a grant proposal with a colleague, gaining $15,000 for teacher training in the Greece Central and Penfield Central School Districts. I also trained more than 60 teachers in the Webster Central School District, where I was coordinator for their K–12 Gifted and Talented Program.

I can't stress enough what a wonderfully powerful and student-oriented writing program Project Success Enrichment is. Children love it and their writing skills improve overnight. Educators love it, too. I know there are many excellent writing programs being marketed, including 6+1 Trait Writing. Once you investigate PSE, however, you'll see this exemplary program has everything 6+1 Trait and other popular writing programs have, plus the powerful element of astounding creativity tied into all the integrative lessons. I asked Executive Director Carolyn Bronson to add an

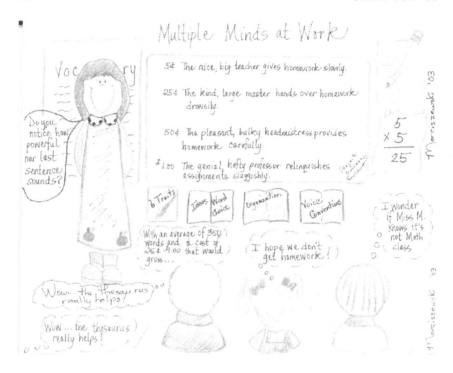

overview here as a guide for your district when considering adoption training of PSE. I've always said, If all our schools trained students K–12 using Project Success Enrichment, our national writing scores would place us in the #1 ranked spot in the world. Project Success is that good! Call or e-mail Carolyn today!

PROJECT SUCCESS ENRICHMENT: A CREATIVE, HANDS-ON EXEMPLARY PROGRAM THAT PROVIDES LITERACY FOR ALL

by Executive Director Carolyn Bronson and
PSE National Trainer Linda Baldwin Ed.D.

Project Success Enrichment (PSE) is a scientifically research-based program that actually meets local, state, and national standards, including No Child Left Behind, while providing teaching strategies and activities for Six Traits Writing Assessment.

PSE is a literacy program that is designed to ensure that *all* students succeed. It was designed using current educational research, theory, and applications in a comprehensive, whole-brain approach. It allows all participants, regardless of their race, age, learning style, or reading level, to achieve success. It is ideal for family literacy and heterogeneous groups including ESL, gifted, and special education students. Each student moves from where he or she is to the next skill level of knowledge in literacy and on to the synthesis and evaluation levels. The PSE curriculum creatively teaches writing basics while developing critical thinking skills and artistic expression.

PSE is also one of the few exemplary, scientifically research-based programs designed for gifted and talented students as evidenced by the catalog of the USOE National Diffusion Network entitled *Educational Programs That Work*. Lessons are presented in a hierarchical sequence from skill awareness through skill acquisition, skill mastery, skill application, to skill transfer. At the skill application level, elaboration, originality, divergent thinking, and problem solving are emphasized. Cooperative learning approaches, such as hands-on activities, shared decision making, active participation, and questioning techniques are demonstrated and experienced throughout the program of activities. Self-management and social skills are also stressed. In this way, culturally embedded cognitive strategies and mediation skills are taught, which provide many at-risk populations with the ability to plan systematically and use new knowledge in alternative settings, and to "own" this new knowledge for future use.

Carolyn Bronson and other educators in a rural school district in Kitsap County, Washington, developed this innovative program in the late 1970s. It was originally used with identified gifted and talented children, including a Native American population, in grades 4–6. In 1983, 1989, and 1996, PSE was validated nationally by the U.S. Department of Education, thus becoming a member of the National Diffusion Network. As a participant in this network, PSE conducts seminars across the nation for educators in grades K–12. The program is implemented in over 2,500 schools in 40 states. It is appropriate for any student population, including a variety of ability levels, learning styles, and cultural backgrounds.

Since PSE incorporates many aspects of traditional Native American education, it is not surprising that it has found so much success in various

Native American communities. PSE teaching techniques allow students to experience learning in their own way and to walk away with their own beliefs about what is and isn't. Because there is no one correct answer, each person's perspective is valued. This is essential to the cognitive development of gifted and talented students, as well as students from a variety of cultural backgrounds.

Accurate, engaging, culturally appropriate literature is used as the foundation for student learning. No reading series is used. Students learn to use reference books to enhance their literacy skills, which means the teacher is not the "all-knowing teller" and that teachers do not "own all important ideas," in what has been referred to as the monistic or didactic system of teaching (Banks and Banks 1993; Garcia 1983). Teachers, parents, and students select appropriate literature to use as the foundation for learning. Cooperative groups, thematic units, self-editing, student-centered assessment, and parent participation are encouraged. In this way, no one person "holds" all the knowledge, but rather knowledge is shared and personalized at a level in which students "own" their own knowledge.

Students learn at their own pace and are not forced into regimented schedules that discourage creativity and concrete understanding of new concepts. Students internalize knowledge in a format that is meaningful and useful to them. Pre- and posttests are built into the curricula. This program uses individualized assessment and is ideal for schools using student portfolios and individualized learning plans. PSE is unique and flexible and can be an effective research-based program for family literacy and after-school and other supplemental educational programs. Students help determine the criteria for assessment and can edit their own work before it is assessed by their peers and teachers. Independent, objective assessment is available for PSE participants to give a more holistic perspective on student achievement.

PSE is a statistically proven program in reading, writing, literary analysis, drawing, painting, and clay work. It uses a portfolio assessment product evaluation that measures the students' growth in language and the visual arts. Evaluation is done by the comparison of pre- and post-student samples collected throughout the year by teachers to be rated by a panel of experts (professional writers or artists and/or English, lan-

guage, or visual arts teachers). PSE has been validated three times as a member of the National Diffusion Network by the U.S. Department of Education.

The average number of sites to adopt PSE has been 276 per year in an average of 22 states. An average of 440 teachers were trained per year, while an average of 36,849 students were affected and served. The results given one school year of instruction (approximately seven months) in grades 3–7 demonstrate more highly developed creative writing skills than those of comparable students. The size of the statistically significant differences and growth, favoring the PSE students, was large in magnitude. They also demonstrated that the levels of significance statistically ranged from $p<.008$ to $p<000$. See table 26.1.

Table 26.1

Year	Training Sessions Conducted	Schools/Sites Adopted Programs	Teachers Trained	Students Served
1989–90	31	201	392	18,106
1990–91	42	312	514	39,064
1991–92	80	300	406	40,019
1992–93	86	326	398	21,628
1993–94	77	301	512	41,216
1994–95	63	218	416	61,602
1995–96	62	281	952	28,560
1996–97	39	204	739	22,170
1997–98	70	200	695	17,375
1998–99	58	406	1450	36,250
1999–2000	60	420	1500	37,500
2000–01	70	357	1275	31,875
2001–02	44	308	1100	27,500
Totals	782	3,834	10,349	422,865

PSE has a training staff of 45, located in various states across the country. The national office is in Seattle, headed by Executive Director/Developer Carolyn Bronson, and offers regional, local, state, and national training. It requires a commitment from the trainers, teachers, and administrators to implement the program on a group or individual basis.

PSE training sessions teach educators of gifted, regular, at-risk, multicultural, ESL, special education, and Chapter One elementary students how to use the PSE Language Arts and/or Visual Arts curriculum. The training program offers basic two- to four-day Level I workshops and indepth, advanced Level II and Level III workshops. Teachers learn a process-oriented approach to the basic curricula and then proceed to advanced units containing more complex projects. The methodology includes lectures, hands-on activities, cooperative learning, problem solving, demonstrations, student samples, brainstorming, and visual aids. Learning to accommodate different learning styles, both academically and cognitively, is emphasized. PSE instructs teachers to use questioning strategies that enhance students' creativity and critical-thinking skills. Teachers learn a structured, organized way to teach writing and thinking skills together, thus connecting the process to reading, literature, and other disciplines. PSE offers an explanation and teaching strategy using the PSE writing process simultaneously with the development of higher-level thinking skills. Teachers learn how to help students organize and plan their literary and/or artistic projects. The workshops can be conducted over one, two, or three years. They may help you develop a new program or stimulate ideas that can be worked into existing programs to enhance teaching. The program accommodates different learning abilities and provides for the *multiple intelligences* and integration people want. Tailor-made workshops for special populations and special levels are also available for groups of 20–30 people. This gradual training program is offered for the following three categories at different levels.

Language Arts

Level I Workshop Offerings:
- Word expansion
- Sentence expansion
- Figurative language
- Nonrhyming poetry
- Descriptive paragraphs
- Writing portfolios
- Editing process

Level II Workshop Offerings:
- Literary elements with descriptive paragraphs
- Rhyming poetry
- Abstract nouns as themes
- Literary analysis
- Editing
- Integration of multidisciplinary themes
- Student product evaluation

Level III Workshop Offerings:
- Symbolism in analysis writing
- Assorted formats for short-story writing
- Integration of different writing styles
- Literature for unit development
- Integration of mechanical and composition skills
- Advanced strategies for questioning and thinking

Visual Arts

Level I Workshop Offerings:
- Basic art elements, techniques, and principles
- Basic drawing techniques—contour, line, and shading
- Basic painting techniques—color, pastels, watercolor
- Basic clay work techniques—pinch, slab pots, and sculpture

Level II Workshop Offerings:
- Basic drawing—hands, faces, three-dimensionality
- Basic painting techniques—color integration, mood painting
- Basic clay work techniques and sculpture

Level III Workshop Offerings:
- Balance with drawing
- Experimentation with multimedia
- Perspective, proportion, texture activities
- Advanced still life
- Geometric design
- Application of advanced art principles and techniques

Integrated Language Arts / Visual Arts

Level I Workshop Offerings:
- Vocabulary development strategies
- Word and sentence expansion
- Contour line with imagery
- Pastel techniques with nonrhyming poetry
- Watercolor techniques with descriptive paragraphs
- Clay work techniques with descriptive paragraphs
- Clay work techniques with characterization
- Art and writing portfolio evaluation

Level II Workshop Offerings:
- Basic line and color techniques
- Use of mixed media
- Drawing techniques using shading
- Question poetry patterns using abstract nouns
- Balance activity and literary analysis
- Development of types of short stories
- Color integration with descriptive paragraphs

Level III Workshop Offerings:
- Symbolism and advanced techniques in art and writing
- Short-story integration and application with visual-art construction
- Multidisciplinary thematic units and projects
- Making connections between literary and artistic elements

In addition, PSE addresses the NCLB regulations and meets local, state, and national standards in a variety of ways:

1. PSE provides a scientifically research-based, highly effective program for most at-risk populations such as ESL, economically disadvantaged, and minority students.

   a. In April 1999, Project Success Enrichment was one out of 26 programs that met stringent criteria for induction into a national project's publication as an example of a content-specific staff development program that increases student achievement (linking teacher learning with student learning). The national project was directed by the National Staff Development Council's Director of Special Projects, Joellen Killion, and involved that organization, along with the NEA, NCTE, NCTS, NASSP, NCTM, ERIC Clearinghouse, and several regional labs. We became a part of their national publication, entitled *Results-Based Staff Development for the Middle Schools: What Works in the Middle.*

   b. In the last year, the National Advisory Panel of the NEA and NSDC's project conducted another review process of over 250 elementary programs. As a result of their efforts, a few of us were chosen to again be a part of their national publication, called *Results-Based Staff Development for the Elementary and High Schools: What Works in the Elementary Grades and High School.*

2. PSE teaches educators how to use alternative, research-based teaching strategies across the curriculum, which reinforces English language development, and reading and writing skills.

3. PSE is a statistically proven program in reading, writing, literary analysis, drawing, painting, and clay work. PSE uses a portfolio assessment product evaluation that measures students' growth in

language and visual arts. PSE provides multiple assessment tools (rubrics) that assist educators with documenting student progress in both art and language arts.

4. PSE provides a variety of whole-brain activities and methods rather than the traditional, ineffective, left-brain-oriented curriculum and teaching techniques.

5. PSE teaches reading, writing, and thinking through art, an effective strategy for teaching right-brained learners that writing can be as creative as art. Art elements, principles, and techniques are used to teach language arts concepts in such a way that students can remember and use writing tools and apply them in other compositions.

6. PSE teaches students how to use reference books (such as a thesaurus for vocabulary development) and does not make the student reliant on the teacher to be the source of information. It also encourages the use of technology to create student products.

7. PSE encourages biculturalism, in that it teaches students who come from cultures that use "circular speak patterns" to use a more standardized format for writing. It teaches them a creative model for writing, which is still descriptive, yet grammatically correct. Also, personification is taught in such a way that it does not conflict with spiritual beliefs in which inanimate objects can have "human-like" qualities.

8. PSE helps students from economically disadvantaged environments to develop cognitive strategies often absent from their learning experiences.

9. PSE helps students from economically disadvantaged environments to learn mediation, which builds cognition.

10. PSE incorporates Gardner's (1999) nine intelligences into the teaching and learning process and provides a training manual that teachers can use for reference. The manual describes all of PSE's programs and key elements. It includes the program's background, history, and original development, as well as explanations of PSE's comprehensive developmental model framework, methodology, and theoretical base. More valuable, however, teachers have information on how to use PSE's diagnostic assessment, identification,

and evaluation tools and procedures. They can immediately implement this information following training. The PSE staff also provides examples of "characteristic sheets," that is, research-based descriptions of various learning styles and explanations (i.e., Gardner's multiple intelligences). In addition, the staff provides examples of student learning in relation to questioning strategies and verb delineations at various levels of creative and critical thinking. These charts, visual aids, and narrative information help the teachers with the use of these strategies in their instructional delivery systems and also give them the tools to use in teaching students how to ask relevant, thought-provoking, probing questions about any topic, theme, idea, or process they may be studying. The PSE developers find these tools to be extremely helpful in developing whole-brain activities related to content.

11. PSE provides an effective platform for family literacy activities. It engages parents and children together in literacy-based art activities, which strengthens the both parent and child's literacy skills.

PSE is especially appropriate for use in programs such as Head Start, Even Start, Title I, Indian Education, and After School programs. It employs program flexibility, allowing multilevel curriculum activities to be used with students of different abilities, including gifted, special education, ESL, regular, ADD, and so forth. PSE produces results and is used in a variety of programmatic models in educational settings.

Project Success offers expertise and staff development to teachers in an area in which they often feel most vulnerable—writing. Project Success is unique in its focus on giving teachers practical strategies for teaching good writing to students of all ages, K–12. These activities focus on word expansion, sentence expansion, figurative language, development of paragraphs, setting description, and character description in just the first level of training. Project Success has several levels of writing instruction, and each gives a whole new set of writing tools. The structure of this program gives success to all students and teachers alike and gives teachers the background to become master writing instructors.

The 6+1 Trait Writing model complements and adds even greater dimension to Project Success. 6+1 Trait Writing is a National Assessment Program that focuses on six or seven characteristics that constitute good writing. Students learn to analyze writing for ideas, organization, voice, word choice, sentence fluency, conventions, and presentation. Using these seven traits, students can learn to look at their own writing from different perspectives. For example, at times the class may assess the finished pieces for organization and conventions, which is the editing aspect of good writing. At other times, a writing piece may be analyzed for the development of sentence fluency or voice. Students learn how to improve each trait in their writing and that makes the whole piece much stronger.

Understanding the language of good writing is most of the battle. Project Success and 6+1 Trait Writing combine to produce students who are fluent in the language of what makes good writing. After students can talk about and identify good writing, daily classroom writing activities become a highlight, not something to be dreaded or avoided as in many middle school classrooms. Both programs give teachers the way to light a fire of excitement and accomplishment in their students

Project Success Enrichment has been implemented in rural, urban, and suburban areas across the country. There are demonstration schools in Texas, Louisiana, Montana, California, New York, New Mexico, Georgia, Delaware, Kentucky, Arizona, North Dakota, South Carolina, Washington, Oklahoma, Colorado, Alabama, and Ohio.

Additional information is available from the PSE National Office in Seattle and on the website www.projse.com. For more information, contact Carolyn Bronson:

Creative Child Concepts
77 Stud Horse Mountain Road
P.O. Box 310
Winthrop, WA 98862
phone: (509) 996-3218
fax: (509) 996-2314
e-mail: bronson@methow.com

(27)

READING COUNTS: BOOK TALK

Marcy Marino

For the next three weeks (approximately), you are going to be reading a book of your choice. This novel should be with you in school at all times so that whenever you have "down time," you can fill it with something educational and fun!

PURPOSE

- To read, have a desire to read, and eventually develop a love for reading.
- To promote your book so your classmates will have a strong desire to read it, too.
- To practice oral presentation skills.
- To compile a list of books recommended by you and your peers for outside reading.

WHAT IS A BOOK TALK?

After reading your book over the next three weeks, you will be asked to perform a one- to two-minute presentation to entice your classmates to read your book. You will be graded on the following aspects of public speaking:

- Eye contact
- Volume
- Pacing
- Posture/gestures
- Clarity/articulation

You may use only one note card with a maximum of 10 words to assist you with your presentation. You will also be graded on how well you promote the book:

- Enthusiasm
- You DO NOT give away the ending or any other important facts in the novel
- Creativity . . . an absolute must!
- You *do* capture the audience's attention and keep it for the entire time

Title of Book: _____

Author: _____

Presentation Option: _____

PRESENTATION OPTIONS

- Try to sell the book . . . dress as a salesman and try to promote the book to a small group of possible consumers (individual)
- Puppet show
- Movie poster . . . promote your novel as a book turned movie (individual)
- Television commercial
- Write a song (individual)
- Create a brochure (individual)

- Newscast
- Dress as the author or one of the characters of the book (individual)
- Dramatize/reenact a scene or two
- Interview a character
- Talk show

If you and a friend would like to read the same novel, it is possible for the two of you to work on one of the options together.

Dear Parent(s) and Guardian(s),

Please be aware that this is an opportunity for your child to take the initiative and create a project that is fun, entertaining, and academic. Although I will occasionally check with your child to make sure he/she is on task with "Reading Counts," your child will be completing the assignment out of class. Therefore, I will need your support at home. Hopefully, by the end of the year, we will have compiled a hearty list of interesting novels and sparked an interest in reading in your child. The list that we compile will be sent home toward the end of the school year so that your child will be able to read, read, read all summer long!

Thank you for your support.

Parent/Guardian Signature: _____

Date: _____

28

SCHOOL-RELATED STUDIES (SRS)

I developed school-related studies (SRS) 15 years ago to help students and parents relate learning as an *ongoing* process occurring naturally, linking their schooltime during the day with their evening at home. Its goal was to reinforce, extend, and enrich learnings presented in school. It has worked equally successfully with 1st graders, 4th graders, middle schoolers, and every age in between.

For a majority of students, the issue of homework had become a negative force rather than the positive educational practice it was originally intended to be—a practice or reinforcement of newly studied objectives. This truly hurt my heart, as learning can be a joyful gift in life. Thus, I invented SRS! SRS is intended to:

- Foster a love of learning in all students
- Promote ongoing learning outside the school setting
- Improve students' independent work habits
- Strengthen communication between home and school
- Raise standards and improve academic performance
- Address individual interests and needs of students at all academic levels

I expected a minimum designated time period to be maintained for SRS after school by all of my students five or six days each week. Parents agreed to help their children select a quiet, well-lighted area where their children could attend to their SRS. They also helped their children make good decisions as they related to their choice of activities. This provided a pleasant, cooperative family planning time together. During SRS, students usually prioritized their work as follows:

1. Complete any unfinished classwork or assignments due the very next day if not completed in allotted school time.
2. Study for upcoming tests, work on long-term projects, and/or review work covered in class.
3. Choose something related to thinking/school topics, which supported academic interests/needs. This could include reading a book of choice, visiting the library, organizing their bedroom, writing a thank-you note, visiting a town board meeting for government, studying for Math Olympiads, or working on an art or Odyssey of the Mind project, to mention just a few.

WHY SRS?

School-related studies allows you to:

- Address individual needs of students at all academic levels
- Help improve students' independent work habits
- Teach students how to learn by using skills such as time management, organization, and good study habits

The suggested minimum time per grade level is as follows:

Grade	Minutes
K	20
1	25
2	30
3	35

4	40
5	50
6	60–75

SRS definitely empowered parents as prime supporters of their children's focused and daily quiet study times at home. It also helped the children focus on daily and long-term assignments. Gone were the previous daily exchanges between parent and child:

"Hi, Johnny. How was your day at school today?"

"OK, Mom."

"Any homework tonight?"

"No, Mom."

Ha! Ha! Home and school become linked with united and similar expectations.

The biggest and most positive change I noticed after the initial transition period into SRS was a significant increase in the amount of pleasure reading my students were doing.

This was true across grade levels. In two or three days, my intermediate students and middle schoolers were polishing off Newbery books and other novels they loved. In fact, at least one-third of my students significantly increased their SRS time voluntarily! Indeed, learning and reading were becoming pleasurable again!

The same was true for my primary students. Reading time increased two-, three-, and fourfold.

Together with positive increases in "attitude toward learning," of equal importance were the increases in test scores and subsequent increases in self-confidence of my SRS students. As part of school-related studies, I required a minimum of 20 percent of SRS to be used three days in a row to study for an upcoming major test. This helped kids get away from cramming the night before a test, helped keep learning from a last-minute review process, and often helped parents become involved with their child in studying for tests.

Enjoyment in learning, increasing test scores, increasing positive self-concept, strengthened home/school connection and communication, reading for pleasure, applicable leanings, etc.—wow, what more could we ask for in a positive and successful school environment?

BRAVO FOR SRS!!!!

Here sits Johnny, capable of Math
problems 6 years beyond grade
level, yet confused by the
simplistic nature of grade level
tests!

㉙

SCRIPPS NATIONAL
SPELLING BEE

I still vividly remember being the first runner-up two years in a row for our local spelling bee in conjunction with the Scripps National Spelling Bee. My picture was in the paper and I was ever so proud. My older brother John was even our district's champion one year. I still use his beautiful engraved dictionary that he received as a first-place winner.

This year, 2005, marks the 78th annual Scripps spelling competition in conjunction with local community newspapers that sponsor a spelling bee program in cooperation with the area schools. Each local champion proceeds to the finals in Washington, DC.

Participating in this spelling bee challenge provides one more way to help children increase their vocabularies, improving their spelling, and enhance their grammar skills. Students under the age of 16 may participate at the local, state, and national levels of competition.

When I became the coordinator for Gifted K–8 in the Webster (N.Y.) Central School District, one of the many activities and programs I helped our schools become involved with was this bee. Children in all seven elementary schools and two middle schools began feverishly studying the word lists from the *Paideia*. This is the "official" spelling book Scripps provides for children to study from. It contains 3,700 words grouped into 26 categories. The good news is this useful study guide only costs $1.50.

Our district champion competed in the regional bee and earned first place. Sarah won a trip to Washington, DC, for herself and her family, to compete in the 1997 national championship. We were all very proud of her and happy with her. Yahoo!

For further information, contact:

Scripps National Spelling Bee
312 Walnut Street, 28th Floor
Cincinnati, OH 45202
www.spellingbee.com
e-mail: Bee@scripps.com

30

SPEAK TO ME ABOUT BEING GIFTED ....

Gifted children talk about . . .

- Being gifted
- Children
- Parents
- Teachers
- School
- Thinking
- America

For years, every summer I coordinated a two-week cultural arts course for gifted 9- to 13-year-olds in our county. The children and I always had a wonderful time together. On the last morning, I would take a peaceful hour with them—soft lights, easy music—and tell the story of Kahlil Gibran's *The Prophet*. I would then ask the children to honor me by being my prophet, answering some of the age-old questions of humankind.

I don't believe I ever underestimated the abilities of my students, but I never ceased to be awed by them.

Following are just a few of the hundreds of responses I received. I'm sure you'll enjoy them as much as the parents and I did.

SPEAK TO ME ABOUT BEING GIFTED

"I like being gifted because it's easy to do things. Sometimes it's frustrating because in school things often seem easy and I like challenges. I especially like problem solving and sharing what I know."
—Emily, age 10

"Being gifted is sometimes annoying because usually I and one other girl in class always know the answers first and are rarely wrong."
—Mara, age 8

"When I was in 2nd grade, I felt trapped, I didn't know why. I would do all the work, but I knew most of it already and it wasn't hard at all. In 3rd grade, I was doing 4th-grade work and I suddenly felt free!"
—Christa, age 9

"I think being gifted means having an IQ of 135 or more."
—Frank, age 9

"Being gifted means to have a talent. Everyone has a talent. It just takes time and practice to achieve it."
—Zach, age 8

"A gifted student is a person who is above the clouds and cannot see the ground from where he started, but can see his destination in the stars."
—Carl, age 11

"To me, it means something special, something unique. You don't need to get great grades or be very smart. You are gifted if you want to touch the sky, if you want to stretch the limit. If you follow your spirit, your heart, your mind, you are gifted."
—Jessica, age 11

"Many people wonder what gifted means. It is my belief that it truly has no specific meaning. It may mean you are talented or smart, or maybe just proud of who you are. You can stretch the limits of this word and make it fit your spirit."
—Kat, age 10

"Gifted means being blessed by God with something special."
—Steven, age 12

CHAPTER 30

SPEAK TO ME ABOUT CHILDREN

"Little children don't really know what is going on in the world and depend on older siblings and parents to guide them. They bring laughter to others because they do funny things."

—Mallory, age 10

"Children are the gift of God."

—JoEllen, age 8

"Children grow up and learn from their mistakes."

—Meghan, age 9

"Children are like the seeds of the future to me. They are the people who will change the world tomorrow and they will succeed in doing so. They are different from adults in a way that they stretch their hands out to the stars and try new things. They are free at heart, mind, and spirit."

—Jessica, age 11

"Children are young adults who have a lot to learn before they grow up."

—Eric, age 10

"Children are little people who haven't learned everything about life. They also make more mistakes than adults."

—Alex, age 10

"Children are all the members of a particular species who have a mother and father."

—Steven, age 12

"Children are people who have very little responsibilities. They can run and play and learn every minute, every instant. They are the plaster, still sifting into the mold, not yet complete."

—Molly, age 10

"A child is anybody who is 18 years old or younger."

—Frank, age 9

"Children are very mentally and physically fragile."

—Andrew, age 11

SPEAK TO ME ABOUT EDUCATION

"You don't have to go to school to have an education. By traveling, exploring, and reading, you can sometimes learn more than you ever could by listening to some lesson given by someone else. Your future depends on your education."

—Katelyn, age 9

"Education is the art of learning."

—Anthony, age 9

SPEAK TO ME ABOUT FRIENDS

"Companion, buddy, could even be a dog or cat."

—Alex, age 8

"Friends are people you can always turn to when something bad happens."

—Mallory, age 10

"People you can tell secrets to and play with."

—Anthony, age 9

"Friends are people who are loyal and true to you. They can be boys or girls. If someone lies to you, he or she shouldn't be your friend."

—Zach, age 8

"A friend is someone who is kind to you and someone you can trust."

—James, age 9

SPEAK TO ME ABOUT PARENTS

"I feel parents help us in life by taking care of us, helping us learn and experience many situations. They are very important to us."

—Andrew, age 9

"Parents are there to support you, help you, teach you, and raise you. Even if your parents get mad at you, they still love you."

—Aaron, age 9

"Sometimes I believe my parents are a curse to me. It seems like they never let me do anything I want—absolutely nothing! Now that I think about it, I guess it is for my own good. If they let me do just about anything I want, I would be extremely spoiled."

—Katelyn, age 9

"My parents are so nice to me, except when I am mean to my sisters. Normally I am nice, so my parents are happy and I enjoy being around them."

—Christa, age 10

"Parents are people who shine lights on the path of life, even though they cannot walk the whole journey with their children."

—Carl, age 11

"Parents are like the sun that nourishes the seed. They love and care for their children, watch them grow, and watch them change the world. Parents bring life into the world and raise it. They are the leaders of their children, who will be the leaders of theirs. They guide us through the hard times, the times when we don't have faith."

—Jessica, age 11

"Parents guide us to our health, our faith, our life. They shape us to be who we are, teach us right from wrong. They are our mothers who brought us onto this earth and the fathers who teach us sports and how to be tough and not to give up. They are our leaders."

—Kat, age 10

"Parents are people who try to do the best for their children."

—Eric, age 10

"Parents are important people because they help children grow and learn so that they can take their rightful places in the world. Without parents, children wouldn't get the nurturing they need."

—Jeffrey, age 11

"Parents are people who can help you when things seem hopeless. Children also reflect their parents."

—Andrew, age 11

"Parents are people who gave you birth and boss you around."

—Katie, age 9

SPEAK TO ME ABOUT SCHOOL

"Schools are where you sit at desks and learn—or relearn."

—Casey, age 9

"School means doing work that is very easy. Because of that, it is often very boring."

—Mary, age 9

"School is a place where average students learn. Gifted students learn anywhere else."

—Carl, age 11

"School is a building filled with learning. It overflows with children who reach to the sky and succeed. It's where friendship sprouts and people come together into one. When I think of a school, a ring of children holding hands and learning comes to mind. School is a building of courage, trying new things, friendship, and learning."

—Jessica, age 11

"School is where people of all ages go to learn new things and be taught the skills that they need in the world."

—Jeffrey, age 11

"School can change the lives of millions because it is the place where teachers teach, the children learn, and the cultural world grows."

—Molly, age 10

"School is a place where children go to learn things to help them in life. Sometimes people who aren't very good in school don't like school and good students like it better."

—Elise, age 11

"School is a place where learning is the key and being with friends is an especially fun part."

—Aileen, age 9

SPEAK TO ME ABOUT TEACHERS

"Teachers are more than just people who tutor you in math, writing, history, etc. They teach you the precious things which will bond with you for as long as you live. Anyone is a teacher: parents, school teachers, friends, even children. They all help us grow joyously and well. Teachers are filled with love and care. They are friends to their students and all who know them."

—Jessica, age 11

"Teachers are people who teach you and help you progress in life. If they are good ones, they will care how you're doing in school."

—Andrew, age 11

SPEAK TO ME ABOUT THINKING

"Thinking is like a seedling that grows through the tangle of my mind. It keeps on flourishing, until it bursts from its shell onto a sheet of paper. Like a waterfall, it keeps on pouring. When a dream forms, I flow with it, wherever it may go. I can travel to the moon if I think about it. Thought is the beginning of a wonderful journey that can take you anywhere in the world."

—Jessica, age 11

"Thinking—What is 2 + 2? If you answered, you were just thinking."

—Kat, age 10

"Thinking is when you use your wits to figure out the answer to a problem."

—Alex, age 10

"Thinking is when anyone in the world has a thought and studies it in their brain. It is how we come up with ideas that make the world better."

—Jeffrey, age 11

"Thinking is what you do when you are trying to figure something out or trying to get an idea."

—Julie, age 10

"Thinking is what you do all the time. You have to think about everything you do. You have to think about what question you want to ask me."

—Ben, age 11

(31)

SQ3R

I don't know how I missed using SQ3R for so many years. It is an invaluable teaching and studying technique. Either I was daydreaming during my undergraduate or graduate education when it was presented or it simply was overlooked. Luckily, I found SQ3R several years ago and use it with my students regularly.

SQ3R is a time-tested and very successful studying technique, which involves *surveying, questioning, reading, reciting,* and *reviewing* materials. Go over this method with your child and help him or her get into the habit of using it to study.

I used SQ3R regularly with my students and it made an amazing difference in their comprehension and achievement test scores.

1. Survey: Look over the entire book, chapter, or whatever content you're going to read. This should include the table of contents, appendixes, author's notes, and similar material.
2. Question: Go over the questions at the end of the chapter or devise your own questions based on what you viewed during your survey. This is especially good for directed reading and study goals and helps keep you focused.

3. Read: Begin reading with your questions actively in your mind. When you find an answer, highlight it or put an asterisk nearby.

4. Recall/recite: Try to recite the important information, definitions, and answers to questions from the material you just read. If you can, good for you! If not, focus and reread the parts you need to and try again. This is an important step that solidifies the material in your brain, making reviewing for tests much easier.

5. Review: This can be done in a variety of ways. You can discuss the material with someone else, checking margin notes, highlighted materials, and underlined sections. Or you can quickly reread, which helps store knowledge in your long-term memory.

32

THE STOCK MARKET GAME

I have loved the Stock Market Game for years. Teams of three to five students compete against each other in sessions of 10 weeks, investing a hypothetical $100,000 in stocks listed on the American and New York Stock Exchanges and the NASDAQ Stock Market. This game is a wonderful, interdisciplinary tool for teachers to integrate lessons in finance and economics in an exciting and motivational way for their students. Student transactions are computed weekly and teams receive weekly financial statements.

The Stock Market Game is available for grades 4–12 and is a national competition. Financial awards are given to the best-performing teams in a geographical area.

Often you can gain access to further information by calling your local newspaper, or contact Gloria Talamas, Stock Market Game director, at:

120 Broadway
New York, NY 10271
(212) 608-1500

You simply can't miss with this integrative activity. Kids love it and learn so much!

SURVIVOR IN ENGLISH 7

Alicia Convery

Objective: Given teacher-assigned sentences, students will decide which literary-device island each sentence belongs on, later voting as a group whether or not it belongs where it is with 100 percent accuracy.

Directions: Create islands from construction paper that are large enough for two to three students to stand on and label them by literary devices. You may want to laminate them for future use. Move desks to the perimeter of the classroom so you have a big open space. Distribute islands evenly across the floor. As students enter the classroom, hand them a sentence in which a literary device is used. They must make decisions individually as to which literary device is used in their sentence and then go and stand on the appropriate island. Once all the students think they have found the correct island, the teacher goes from island to island and has the class decide or vote on whether or not each student is in the correct place.

Pros: Attractive to kinestic and interpersonal learners. Teacher has control of difficulty level when he or she passes out the sentences. Learners are pushed to different levels without being blatantly classified into ability groups. Lesson can be modified to fit several curricula.

Cons: Voting can get boring and easier questions can lose the attention of gifted students.

TINY WORLDS

Greg K. Szulgit

Most animals and fungi (and many plants) are much smaller than we are. So, it is easy for us to overlook many of the important factors that affect life for these creatures. The purpose of this exercise is to get students thinking about the concept of tiny habitats. The closer they look, the more they will be able to find tiny habitats that exist within other habitats. Think about a patch of grass, for example: we might think that it is just one habitat. But, when you look closely, you will find that there are lots of tiny environments in just that one small area. The dirt might be cool and damp, while the top of the grass might be dry and warm. The stems of the grass are under the leaves, or "blades," and are often in the shade, while the leaves themselves might be exposed to strong sunlight all day long.

The assignment is for the students to find an outdoor space of their own choosing that is approximately the size of their hand. They should begin by drawing this space in detail (using colored pencils). The drawing should take them quite some time, as they should record every detail possible. The more time they spend observing the details, the more they will appreciate the tiny little world within this space. As they draw their space, they should consider the following parameters and how they change from one tiny space to the next:

- light
- heat
- water/moisture
- fresh air
- food
- colors
- any other parameters that they can think of (like movement of the surroundings)

Now they should describe several mini-environments that they have found within this area (e.g., they might describe the underside of a leaf as one environment, while the top side of the leaf is a very different environment—in what ways do they differ?). They should dedicate a paragraph to each parameter or mini-environment.

Finally, they should spend a few paragraphs describing all of the creatures (not just the animals) that are present. Why do they think they are located where they are, and how do they think each creature deals with its mini-environment? How do they suppose the various creatures interact with each other?

As usual, both teachers and students might want to modify the assignment a bit to fulfill their own interests.

35

WEB QUESTS AND THE GIFTED: CHURCHVILLE–CHILI CENTRAL SCHOOL DISTRICT

Kerry Williams

While every child's education is important, what happens to gifted children who go unrecognized in a classroom where lessons are below their intellectual ability? Unfortunately, this occurs in far too many classrooms in the United States. It is reported that students who are above their peers intellectually sit through already learned material 30 percent of the time. Those gifted students, furthermore, waste even more time.

Web quests are a wonderful way to differentiate curriculum. The teacher provides the assignment and it is placed online for all students to see and use. Web quests are available for any given subject and are created toward "real life" applications. Creating a web quest is fairly simple: teachers assign a lesson that enables them to give the "task," "process," and "evaluation" aspects of the assignment. Other links can be created to enhance the material, whether for research information, models, or webs to get a student started.

The short-story web quest we have completed in the Churchville–Chili (N.Y.) Central School District has been designed for this purpose. The task asks the student to write an original short story for possible publication in any of our national publication sites. Students can choose to write for *Cupid's Corner*, *Whodunit?*, *Action!*, or *Alien Chronicles*. All exemplary work is then posted online for other to read and evaluate.

This has been motivating for all students, especially those gifted students who strive for leadership and creative efforts to be recognized.

The process page is designed to outline what is expected in the assignment. Students should compose a story that contains basic plot elements, along with setting, point of view, characterization, protagonist and antagonist, and a conflict. They are also expected to successfully incorporate any of the literary elements found in literature. They are, again, given the opportunity to use any they feel comfortable with, including mood, irony, foreshadowing, imaginary, personification, symbolism, and simile/metaphors. Those with higher intellectual ability will strive to use any of these in their own writing and may extend them throughout their writing.

All students are encouraged to use dialogue in their short stories. This is an assignment where students can cooperatively work together to create different characters, follow up others' work with sequels, or tackle individual writing, which can be more challenging.

Gifted students are able to see how they will be graded from the evaluation page that is also a part of the web quest. This rubric is formulated in correspondence with the New York State Standards. Each concept is evaluated on a four-point scale, and the rubric expectations encourage students' creativity by using meaning, development, organization, story elements, literacy elements, and language use.

When I used the short-story web quest with my students last year, I had phenomenal results. My most talented students shone with brilliance in their own writing. The stories were creative, interactive, and publishable. We celebrated our writing with a day in front of the "campfire," and all students were encouraged to share their writing.

For more information, please contact Kerry at Kwilliams@cccsd.org.

A

PROFESSIONAL ASSOCIATIONS AND ADVOCACY GROUPS

Association for the Gifted, a division of the Council for Exceptional Children; 1110 North Glebe Road, Suite 300; Arlington, VA 22201; (703) 620-3660

Missouri Department of Education, Gifted Education Programs; P.O. Box 480; Jefferson City, MO 65102; (573) 751-2453

Frances A. Karnes Center for Gifted Studies; University of Southern Mississippi, Box 8207; Hattiesburg, MS 39406; (601) 266-5236

American Mensa, Ltd.; 1229 Corporate Drive West; Arlington, TX 76006; (817) 607-0060

National Association for Creative Children and Adults; 8080 Springvalley Drive; Cincinnati, OH 43236; (513) 631-1777

National Association for Gifted Children; 1707 L Street, NW, Suite 1002; Washington, DC 20036; (202) 785-4268

National Association of State Boards of Education; 277 S. Washington Street, Suite 100; Alexandria, VA 22314; (703) 684-4000

Supporting Emotional Needs of the Gifted; P.O. Box 6074; Scottsdale, AZ 85261; (773) 857-6250

Talent Identification Program, Duke University; 1121 West Main Street, P.O. Box 90780; Durham, NC 27708; (919) 668-9100

World Council for Gifted and Talented Children; 18401 Hiawatha Street; Northridge, CA 91326; (818) 368-7501

ADDITIONAL RESOURCES

Association for the Education of Gifted Underachieving Students (AE-GUS); P.O. Box 221; Mountain Lakes, NJ 07046

National Research Center on the Gifted and Talented; University of Connecticut; 2131 Hillside Road, Unit 3007; Storrs, CT 06269; (860) 486-4676

Parent Information Network for the Gifted (PING); 190 Rock Road; Glen Park, NJ 07542-1736; (900) 773-7464

USEFUL TEACHING TOOLS AND RESOURCES FOR TEACHERS

Internet Websites

www.ABCTEACH.com: This site is awesome, containing lesson plans, thematic units, printables, center signs, awards, and certificates. Just type in your topic and ideas pop up!

www.about.com: This has a huge variety of items—crafts, coloring sheets, etc. Invaluable resources.

www.aboutourkids.org: Deals with children's issues.

www.ala.org: This is a super site, having tons or booklists arranged in various ways by age level group topic and genre. It also provides excellent materials for parents, teachers and students themselves. It further offers an extensive list of links to other sites . . . a terrific resource.

www.angelfire.com/mi/psociety/: The page of procrastination.

www.audible.com: Audible is a monthly subscription service where you can download audiobooks. Storing these on a computer or burning them to a disk and allowing students to listen to the books as they read is an excellent tool for the reluctant reader. While the teen section is limited, it is good for older readers. Poetry drama and short stories are included. It costs $21.95 a month and allows you two downloads per month. Comparatively, those audiobooks cost between $30 and $70 in a retail store.

www.bookadventure.com: This offers quizzes pertaining to popular literature stories.

www.discovery.com: This is an excellent resource for teachers with awesome information for students. It is linked to shows with activities online and lesson plan ideas. Simply great!

www.englishcompanion.com: Composed by teachers, filled with creative lesson and organizers.

www.eparent.com: *Exceptional Parent* magazine's online resource providing information, support, and ideas to families of children with disabilities.

www-epgy.stanford.edu: The Education Program for Gifted Youth (EPGY) at Stanford University is a continuing project dedicated to developing and offering multimedia computerized distance learning courses. Through EPGY, students have access to courses in a variety of subjects at levels ranging from kindergarten through advanced undergraduate. Currently more than 3,000 students from 28 countries are enrolled in EPGY.

www.ericec.org: Information Center on Disabilities and Gifted Education.

www.eriecanal.org: This website is dedicated to the history of the New York State Erie Canal.

familyeducation.com/home/: Family education network.

www.freeworksheets.com: Promoted as the Web's leading source of educational content and resources and shopping for parents, teachers, and kids. This is a great resource for ideas on units, chat rooms, and more.

www.funbrain.com and www.factmonster.com: Both websites offer online activities related to writing for students. One very popular game is Grammar Gorillas, a fun way of quizzing your knowledge of the parts of speech. They also offer quizzes on popular pieces of literature, vocabulary activities, and puzzles.

www.gifted.org: The Gifted Child Society is a nonprofit organization that was founded in 1957 by parents in New Jersey and furthers the cause of gifted children. The society has served over 60,000 children and their families.

www.hoagiesgifted.org: Hoagies' gifted education page. "Who dares to teach must never cease to learn" (John Cotton Dan). This website is loaded with resources and valuable links!

www.hurricanehunters.com: Photos and information from the Hurricane Hunters of the Air Force Reserve. Take a "cyberflight" and follow them on a trip.

www.jhu.edu/~gifted/: The Johns Hopkins University Center for Talented Youth.

www.kidsdomain.com: This website is wonderful because it offers many activities and ideas for all age groups. It offers ideas for kids, parents, teachers, and others. Another great feature is that this site has important monthly information, for example, the history of Flag Day. This is a great website!

www.kz.com: This site coordinates with a math series. Students have their screen names and passwords, playing games and practicing math problems. Parents and teachers can log on and see the students' progress. Students can earn points to play secret games.

www.middleweb.com: Explores middle school reform.

www.msrogers.com: Poetry and creative lessons.

www.nagc.org: This takes you to the National Association for Gifted Children's home page—filled with information on national educator awards, student awards, competitions, grants, other awards and continuing education opportunities.

www.naspcenter.org: National Association of School Psychologists' National Mental Health and Education Center website contains information about how to cope with teenagers.

notmykid.org: Practical parenting solutions.

parenthoodweb.com: an award-winning online parenting, pregnancy, and family community resource for parents and prospective parents. Free expert advice, discussion groups and chat, polls, recall information, and birth announcements.

www.peacecorps.com: This site offers lessons pertaining to different ethnic groups/areas, using multicultural literature and learnings about other cultures.

www.poetry180.com: Excellent for modern poetry and very student friendly.

www.proteacher.com: Offers a variety of ideas, across all content areas and specific to grade levels. Can read letters from other teachers for ideas on specific lessons.

www.rainbow.org: This has tons of great songs and activities for the elementary level.

www.scholasticnews.com: Students can read *Scholastic News* magazine in class, then take a quiz on the reading to measure their comprehension. This activity provides a good review of current events.

www.SenecaParkzoo.com: Kids absolutely love it! While these websites are more localized for western New York teachers, using them allows classes to explore different science units in depth and create a larger interest level for them. Excellent motivator preceding an actual field trip to the zoo in Rochester.

www.southwest.com/adoptapilot: Adopt-a-Pilot program. What: Southwest Airlines' mentoring program that pairs pilots with fifth-grade pupils around the country, many in cities the airline doesn't even serve. How: Pilots meet with pupils in the classroom and stay in touch during their travels. The program is free.

www.teachertools.org: A helpful site containing many types of form letters and templates to use.

www.teach-nology.com: Rubric maker—what more can I say! Enjoy saving time with this website! This site has rubrics that you can create by just plugging in your information. Wonderful asset for evaluation!

www.tagfam.org: TAG Families of the Talented and Gifted has a positive outlook on life and living. In 1994, Valorie King created a charter list to serve as an online support community for talented and gifted individuals and their families. The TAG FAM mailing list is host to a supportive community, which by design mixes both informative posting and personal sharing in response to the problems and situations that motivate individuals to participate.

www.ucon.edu/nrcgt.html: National Resource Center on the Gifted and Talented (NRCG/T). The mission of this center is to plan and conduct a program of high quality that is theory-driven, problem-based, practice-relevant, and consumer-oriented, with a broad-based dissemination function that targets practitioners, parents, policy makers, and researchers. NRCG/T is funded by the Jacob K. Javits Gifted and Talented Students' Education Act.

www.weatherwizkids.com: Designed to give kids a look into the fascinating world of weather. Includes games, quizzes, and experiments they can do at home.

www.webenglishteacher.com: Great resource for any literature unit/lesson. It provides printouts, lessons, units, activities, links to other sources, summaries, review questions, and analysis.

www.yahoo.com/text/education/k_12/gifted_youth: Yahoo Resources for Gifted Youth K–12. Filled with dozens of excellent resources on the topic of gifted and talented.

www.yahooligans.com: This word game so great! Kids love it and it's great for spelling and building vocabulary skills/sight words.

Journals and Magazines

Creative Child and Adult Quarterly; 8080 Springvalley Drive; Cincinnati, OH 45236; (513) 631-1777

Gifted Child Quarterly; NAGC; 1707 L Street, NW, Suite 550; Washington, DC 20036; (202) 785-4268

Gifted Child Today; P.O. Box 8813; Waco, TX 76714; (800) 998-2208

Journal of Creative Behavior; Creative Education Foundation; 289 Bay Road; Hadley, MA 01035

Journal for the Education of the Gifted; official publication of the Association for the Gifted, a division of the Council for Exceptional Children; 1110 North Glebe Road, Suite 300; Arlington, VA 22201; (703) 620-3660

Mensa Research Journal; 1229 Corporate Drive West; Arlington, TX 76006; (817) 607-0060

Parenting for High Potential; NAGC; 1707 L Street, NW, Suite 550; Washington, DC 20036; (202) 785-4268

Roeper Review; Roeper Institute; P.O. Box 329; Bloomfield Hills, MI 48303-0329; (313) 642-1500

STATE ORGANIZATIONS

Alabama Association for Gifted Children: www.aagc.freeservers.com/
   aagc.html
Arizona Association for Gifted and Talented: www.azagt.org
Arizona Association for the Gifted: www.aagt.org
Arkansans for Gifted and Talented Education: pollyb@af.affc.k12.ar.us
California Association for the Gifted (CAG): www.CAGifted.org
Colorado Association for the Gifted: CAGT@aol.com
Connecticut Association for the Gifted and Talented: www.CTGifted.org
Delaware Talented and Gifted Association: mdee@state.de.us
Florida Association for the Gifted (FLAG) and Parents for Able Learner
   Students: members.aol.com/pals222
Georgia Association for Gifted Children: www.gagc.org
Hawaii Gifted Association: tel. (808) 732-1138
Idaho—The Association for the Gifted (ITAG): coehp.idbsu.edu/
   itagsage
Illinois Association for Gifted Children (IAGC): IAGCGifted.org
Indiana Association for the Gifted: www.iag-online.org
Iowa Talented and Gifted Association: www.uiowa.edu/~itag
Kansas Association for the Gifted, Talented, and Creative: www.KGTC.org
Kentucky Association for Gifted Education (KAGE): www.wku.edu/
   KAGE
[Louisiana] Association for Gifted and Talented Students (AGTS):
   hal.calc.k12.la.us/~gifted/gifted.html
Maine Educators Gifted and Talented (MEGAT): www.sad28.k12.me.us
Maryland Coalition for Gifted and Talented Education: jroache@ids2
   .idsonline.com
Massachusetts Association for Gifted Education (MAGE): www.MASS
   Gifted.org
Michigan Alliance for Gifted Education (MAGE): www.migiftedchild.org
Minnesota Council for the Gifted and Talented: www.MCGT.net
Minnesota Educators of the Gifted and Talented: www.informns.k12
   .us/~megt
Mississippi Association for Gifted Children (MAGC): www.magc.org
[Missouri] Gifted Association of Missouri (GAM): www.mogam.org

Montana Association of Gifted and Talented Education: www
.members.home.net/cabreras/agate.htm

Nebraska Association for the Gifted: www.NebraskaGifted.org

Nevada Association for Gifted and Talented (NAGT): tel. (775) 852-
8209, asprinkle@washoe.k12.nv.us

New Hampshire Association for Gifted Children: tel. (603) 882-3512,
Gifteacher@aol.com

New Jersey Association for Gifted Children: www.NJAGC.org

New Mexico: psutcliffe@sde.state.nm.us

[New York] Advocacy for Gifted and Talented Education in New York
(AGATE): www.agateny.org

North Carolina Association for the Gifted and Talented (NCAGT):
www.ncagt.org

North Dakota: jkolberg@state.nd.us

Ohio Association for Gifted Children (OAGC): www.oagc.com

Oklahoma Association for Gifted, Creative, and Talented: tel. (405) 262-
2765

Oregon Association for Talented and Gifted (OATAG): www.oatag.org

Pennsylvania Association for Gifted Education (PAGE): www
.penngifted.org

Rhode Island—Gifted and Talented: www.ri.net/gifted_talented/rhode
.html

South Carolina Consortium for Gifted Education: www.SCCGE.org

South Dakota Association for Gifted Education: tel. (605) 394-4031,
silvermn@rapidnet.com

Tennessee Association for the Gifted (TAG): www.tag-tenn.org

Texas Association for the Gifted and Talented (TAGT): www.txgifted.org

Utah Association for Gifted Children (UAGC): www.uagc.org

Vermont Network for the Gifted: tel. (802) 985-3405

Virginia Association of the Gifted (VAG): www.vagifted.org

Washington Association of Educators of the Talented and Gifted
(WAETG): www.WAETG.org

[Washington] Northwest Gifted Child Association: www.innw.net/explor-
ers/nwgac.htm

West Virginia Association for Gifted and Talented: www.geocities.com/
athens/olympus/4764/wvagt.html

Wisconsin Association for Gifted and Talented (WATG): www.focol.org/
~watg

MAGAZINES THAT PUBLISH CHILDREN'S WORKS

Creative Kids

Creative Kids magazine is the nation's largest magazine by and for
kids. The magazine bursts with games, stories, and opinions—all by and
for kids ages 8–14. In the pages of *Creative Kids* you will find such fun
activities as: brain teasers, contests, stories, poetry, pen pals, mysteries,
and much more! This interactive magazine also includes activities that
stimulate and encourage the creativity of readers.

Kids from all over the world read and contribute to *Creative Kids*.
The magazine includes exciting examples of the most creative student
work to be found in any publication. Kids express themselves in letters
to the editor, answers to posed questions, and questions of their own.
www.prufrock.com

Stone Soup

A magazine by young writers and artists (ages 8–13), *Stone Soup* is
unique among children's magazines—it's the only one made up entirely of
the creative work of children. Young people from all over the world contribute their stories, poems, book reviews, and artwork to it. The magazine is published six times a year—January, March, May, July, September,
and November—and contains no advertising. www.stonesoup.com

Skipping Stones

Skipping Stones is a nonprofit children's magazine that contains stories, articles, and photos from all over the world. The magazine accepts
art and original writing in all languages and from all ages. Non-English
writings are accompanied by English translations to encourage the
learning of other languages. Each issue also contains international pen
pals, book reviews, news, and a guide for parents and teachers. Published bimonthly during the school year. www.skippingstones.org

Cicada

A literary magazine for teenagers and young adults (ages 14 and up), *Cicada* publishes original short stories, poems, and first-person essays and encourages submissions from its readers. It's published six times per year. www.cicadamag.com

Kidnews.com

Kidnews.com is a free news and writing service for students and teachers from around the globe and has published thousands of young authors from every continent (except Antarctica)! Anyone may submit a review, journalism piece, short story, poem, sports critique, real-life account, opinion piece, or advice to fellow kids. Every submission, just like at a publishing house, is edited and reviewed for content and language before being posted. Kids can also find a pen pal on this site. www.kidnews.com

STATE DEPARTMENT OF EDUCATION GIFTED EDUCATION CONTACTS (AS OF 12/01/03)

Alabama Department of Education; P.O. Box 302101; Montgomery, AL 36130-2101; (334) 242-8114; (334) 242-9192 (fax)

Alaska Department of Education and Early Development; 801 West 10th Street, Suite 200; Juneau, AK 99801; (907) 465-8727; (907) 465-6760 (fax)

Arizona Department of Education; 1535 West Jefferson Street; Phoenix, AZ 85007; (602) 364-4017; (602) 542-3100 (fax)

Arkansas Department of Education; Education Bldg., Room 203-B; 4 Capitol Mall; Little Rock, AR 72201; (501) 682-4224; (501) 682-4220 (fax)

California Department of Education; 1430 N Street, Suite 2401; Sacramento, CA 95814; (916) 323-5505

Colorado Department of Education; 201 East Colfax Avenue; Denver, CO 80203-1799; (303) 866-6652; (303) 866-6811 (fax)

Connecticut Department of Education; 165 Capitol Avenue, Room 205; Hartford, CT 06106; (860) 713-6745; (860) 713-7018 (fax)

Delaware Department of Education; P.O. Box 1402; John G. Townsend Building; Dover, DE 19903; (302) 739-4885, ext. 3145; (302) 739-4675 (fax)

Florida Department of Education; 614 Turlington Building; 325 W. Gaines Street; Tallahassee, FL 32399-0400; (850) 245-0478; (850) 922-7088 (fax)

Georgia Department of Education; 1770 Twin Towers East; Atlanta, GA 30334-5040; (404) 657-0182; (404) 657-7096 (fax)

Guam Department of Education; P.O. Box DE; Hagåtña, Guam 96932; (671) 475-0598

Hawaii Department of Education; 637 18th Avenue, Bldg. C, #204; Honolulu, HI 96816; (808) 733-4476; (808) 733-4475 (fax)

Idaho Department of Education; P.O. Box 83720; Boise, ID 83720-0027; (208) 332-6920

Illinois Board of Education; 100 North First Street, #205; Springfield, IL 62777; (217) 782-2826

Indiana Department of Education; Room 229, State House; Indianapolis, IN 46204; (317) 233-5191; (317) 232-9121 (fax)

Iowa Department of Education; Grimes State Office Building; East 14th & Grand; Des Moines, IA 50319-0146; (515) 281-3199; (515) 242-6025 (fax)

Kansas Department of Education; 120 SE 10th Avenue; Topeka, KS 66612; (785) 291-3097; (785) 296-1413 (fax)

Kentucky Department of Education; Division of Professional Development; 500 Mero Street, Room 1835; Frankfort, KY 40601; (502) 564-2106 ext. 4137

Louisiana Department of Education; 1453 Patrick Drive; Baton Rouge, LA 70810; (225) 342-5295; (225) 342-3281 (fax)

Maine Department of Education; 23 State House Station; Augusta, ME 04333; (207) 624-6831; (207) 624-6821 (fax)

Maryland Department of Education; 200 West Baltimore Street; Baltimore, MD 21201-2595; (410) 767-0363; (410) 333-2050 (fax)

Massachusetts Department of Education; 350 Main Street; Malden, MA 02148; (781) 338-6239

Michigan Department of Education; P.O. Box 30008; Lansing, MI 48909; (517) 373-4213; (517) 241-0197 (fax)

Minnesota Department of Education; Office of Teaching and Learning; Children, Families, and Learning Department; 1500 Highway 36 West; Roseville, MN 55113-4266; (651) 582-8812

Mississippi Department of Education; Office of the Deputy Superintendent; P.O. Box 771; Jackson, MS 39205-0771; (601) 359-2588; (601) 359-2326 (fax)

Missouri Department of Elementary and Secondary Education; P.O. Box 480; Jefferson City, MO 65102; (573) 751-2453; (573) 751-9434 (fax)

Montana Office of Public Instruction; P.O. Box 202501; Helena, MT 59620-2501; (406) 444-4317; (406) 444-1373 (fax)

Nebraska Department of Education; 301 Centennial Mall South, Box 94987; Lincoln, NE 68509-4987; (402) 471-0737; (402) 471-8850 (fax)

Nevada Department of Education; 700 E. Fifth St.; Carson City, NV 89701; (775) 687-9142; (775) 775-9101

New Hampshire Department of Education; 101 Pleasant Street; Concord, NH 03301; (603) 271-1536; (603) 271-1953 (fax)

New Jersey Department of Education; Legge House, Normal Avenue; Montclair State University; Upper Montclair, NJ 07043; (973) 569-2113

New Mexico Public Education Department; 300 Don Gaspar; Santa Fe, NM 87501; (505) 827-6653; (505) 827-6791(fax)

New York State Education Department; Room 981 EBA; Washington Avenue; Albany, NY 12234; (518) 474-8773

North Carolina Department of Public Instruction; 6356 Mail Service Center; Raleigh, NC 27699-6356; (919) 807-3987; (919) 807-3243 (fax)

North Dakota Department of Public Instruction; State University Station, Box 5036; Fargo, ND 58105-5036; (701) 231-6030

Ohio Department of Education; 25 S. Front Street; Mailstop 205; Columbus, OH 43215; (614) 752-1221; (614) 752-1429 (fax)

Oklahoma Department of Education; 2500 N. Lincoln Blvd., Suite 316; Oklahoma City, OK 73105-4599; (405) 521-4287; (405) 521-2971 (fax)

Oregon Department of Education; 255 Capitol Street, NE; Salem, OR 97310-0290; (503) 378-3598 ext. 640

Pennsylvania Department of Education; Bureau of Special Education, 7th Floor; 333 Market Street; Harrisburg, PA 17126-0333; (717) 783-6881

Rhode Island Department of Elementary and Secondary Education; 255 Westminister Street, Room 400; Providence, RI 02903-3400; (401) 222-4600, ext. 2318; (401) 222-6030 (fax)

South Carolina Department of Education; 1429 Senate Street, Room 801; Columbia, SC 29201; (803) 734-8335; (803) 734-6142 (fax)

South Dakota Department of Education; 700 Governors Drive; Pierre, SD 57501-2291; (605) 773-4662; (605) 773-3782 (fax)

Tennessee Department of Education; Division of Special Education; 710 James Robertson Parkway, 8th Floor; Nashville, TN 37243-0380; (615) 741-7811; (615) 532-9412 (fax)

Texas Education Agency; 1701 N. Congress Avenue; Austin, TX 78701-1494; (512) 463-9455

Utah Office of Education; P.O. Box 144200; Salt Lake City, UT 84114-4200; (801) 538-7884; (801) 538-7769 (fax)

Vermont Department of Education; 120 State Street; Montpelier, VT 05620-2501; (802) 828-5411

Virginia Department of Education; Office of Elementary and Middle School; P.O. Box 2120; Richmond, VA 23218-2120; (804) 225-2884; (804) 786-1703 (fax)

Washington Office of Public Instruction; P.O. Box 47200; 600 South Washington; Olympia, WA 98504-7200; (360) 725-6100; (360) 586-3305 (fax)

Washington, DC, Public Schools; 825 N. Capitol Street, NE, Room 8084; Washington, DC 20002; (202) 442-5650

West Virginia Department of Education; Capitol Complex; Building 6, Room 304; Charleston, WV 25305; (304) 558-2696; (304) 558-3741 (fax)

Wisconsin Department of Public Instruction; P.O. Box 7841; Madison, WI 53707; (615) 266-2364

Wyoming Department of Education; Hathaway Building, 2nd Floor; 2300 Capitol Avenue; Cheyenne, WY 82002; (307) 777-5217

(B)

CONTESTS

THE *CONCORD REVIEW* EMERSON PRIZE

The *Concord Review* is a quarterly journal that publishes history papers written by high school students. Since 1987, the *Concord Review* has published 649 student papers from 43 states and 33 other countries. The Ralph Waldo Emerson Prizes for student work of outstanding academic promise at the secondary level are chosen from the authors published in the journal during the previous year. Essays are accepted on a rolling admission basis. Essays can be on any historical topic and the length should be 4,000–6,000 words with endnotes. Each essay must be typed and printed from a word processor. Each entry must be accompanied by a check for $40 and the entry form. For more information, contact Will Fitzhugh, Editor, *Concord Review*, 730 Boston Post Road, Suite 24, Sudbury, MA 01776; call (800) 331-5007 or (978) 443-0022; e-mail fitzhugh@tcr.org; or visit www.tcr.org.

THE INTEL® SCIENCE TALENT SEARCH

The Intel® Science Talent Search, previously known as the Westinghouse Science Talent Search, is America's oldest precollege science contest. Eligible students include high school seniors in the United States and its territories, and American students attending school abroad. Each year, almost 2,000 students accept the challenge of completing an entry for the Intel Science Talent Search, with finalists competing for the top prize of a $100,000 scholarship. Each student completes a written description of his or her research, plus an entry form that encourages student creativity and interest in science. Search candidates are judged by a board of 10 distinguished scientists from a variety of disciplines. The top 300 entrants are selected as semifinalists. Intel and Science Service recommend these students to colleges and universities for admission and financial assistance. Forty top contenders are announced in January with final judging in March. For more information, write Science Service, 1719 N Street, NW, Washington, DC 20036; call (202) 785-2255; fax (202) 785-1243; or visit www.sciserv.org.

NATIONAL ARBOR DAY POSTER CONTEST

Fifth-grade students in states represented by a National Arbor Day state coordinator are eligible to compete. Each state selects a winner. From among the state winners, one national winner is selected. The national winner, his or her parents, and the teacher of the winning student receive an expense-paid trip to Nebraska City, Nebraska, home of Arbor Day, and participate in April National Awards Weekend. The national winner also receives a $1,000 savings bond and a lifetime membership in the National Arbor Day Foundation. The winning teacher receives $200 for classroom materials. The national second-place winner receives a $500 savings bond, and the third-place winner receives a $250 bond. Teachers of the second- and third-place winners receive $100 and $50, respectively. For more information, contact the National Arbor Day Foundation, Poster Contest Coordinator, P.O. Box 85784, Lincoln, NE 68501-5784; e-mail education@arborday.org; or visit www.arborday.org/kids/postercontest.html.

MUSIC TEACHERS NATIONAL ASSOCIATION STUDENT COMPETITION

The Music Teachers National Association (MTNA) Student Competitions consist of three levels: state competition, division competition, and national finals. Teachers may enter only students who are currently studying an instrument, voice, or composition with them in competitions. For more information, contact MTNA headquarters, 441 Vine Street, Suite 505, Cincinnati, OH 45202-2811; call (888) 512-5278; fax (513) 421-2503; e-mail mtnanet@mtna.org; or visit www.mtna.org/scap .htm.

C

GRANTS AND AWARDS

HASBRO CHILDREN'S FOUNDATION

The Hasbro Children's Foundation funds development and expansion of programs serving economically disadvantaged children under age 13. Programs must provide direct services and serve as replicable models. The Hasbro Playspaces initiative funds fully integrated, universally accessible playgrounds allowing children with disabilities ages 2–12 access to 70–100 percent of its play events and activities. Priority goes to playgrounds serving low-income communities. There are no deadlines. Apply no more than once a year. Grants for local model programs range from $500–35,000. For more information, contact Hasbro Children's Foundation, 32 W. 23rd Street, New York, NY 10010; call (917) 606-6226; or visit www.hasbro.org.

ALLIANT ENERGY FOUNDATION

The Alliant Energy Foundation makes education grants in its communities. Grants support youth mentoring and minority enrichment. October 1 is the deadline. Apply online. For more information, contact Alliant Energy Foundation, 222 W. Washington Ave., Madison, WI 53703;

Alliant Energy Foundation, 200 1st Street, SE, Cedar Rapids, IA 52401; call (800) ALLIANT; or visit http://www.alliantenergy.com.

THE NATIONAL INSTITUTES OF HEALTH

The National Institutes of Health are funding science education partnership grants, designed to help scientists work with educators and local organizations to boost K–12 students' understanding of science and health. Deadline is October 1. Grants can be of any size up to $300,000. For more information, contact Paul Karadbil, National Institutes of Health, at (301) 435-0844, or e-mail paulk@ncrr.nih.gov.

LOWE'S

Lowe's Foundation Education funds small-scale products near their stores. The foundation considers any type of education based on community needs and store managers' expertise. Funding levels vary depending on your school's proposal. Managers accept applications anytime. For more information, contact David Loiver, Lowe's Foundation, at (333) 658-4000, or visit lowes.com.

NATIONAL ENDOWMENT FOR THE HUMANITIES

The National Endowment for the Humanities assists educators with professional development activities with content-rich technology resources in the classroom. It helps teachers in elementary, middle, or high schools who study core subjects with professors at colleges and universities. Deadline is October 1. Grants can be of any size up to $100,000. For more information, contact the National Endowment for the Humanities, (202) 606-8380; e-mail education@neh.gov; or visit www.neh.gov.

ADVANCED TECHNOLOGICAL EDUCATION

The Advanced Technological Education program promotes improvement in technological education at the secondary-school levels by supporting curriculum development; the preparation and professional development of college faculty and secondary-school teachers; internships and field experiences for faculty, teachers and students; and other activities. Deadline is October 16. An estimated 70 awards are funded from a $39 million fund. For more information, contact the National Science Foundation Advanced Technological Education Program at (703) 292-8668 or e-mail undergrad@nsf.gov.

CORNING FOUNDATION

The Corning Foundation offers awards for community service, curriculum, student awards, administration, and technology. Projects create partnerships between educational, cultural, community, and selected national organizations and elementary and secondary schools, community colleges, and four-year colleges. Past projects have included community-service programs for students, curriculum enrichment, student scholarships, facility improvement, and instructional technology projects for the classroom. The website provides this year's deadlines. For more information, contact Kristin Swain, Corning Foundation, at (607) 974-9000, or visit www.corning.com.

REFERENCES AND RECOMMENDED READING

Ablard, K. E., & Parker, W. D. (1997). Parents' achievement goals and perfectionism in their academically talented children. *Journal of Youth and Adolescence, 26,* 65–66.

Ableman, R. (1992). *Some children under some condition: TV and the high potential kid.* Storrs: University of Connecticut, The National Research Center on the Gifted.

Adderholdt, M. R., & Goldberg, J. (1999). *Perfectionism: What's bad about being too good?* Minneapolis: Free Spirit.

Allen, R., Skitt, C., & Gale, H. (1994). *Mensa publications: Mighty mindbenders.* Austin, TX: Barnes & Noble Books.

Archambault, F., Westberg, K., Brown, S., Hallmark, B., Zhang, W., & Emmons, C. (1993). Classroom practices used with gifted third and fourth grade students. *Journal for the Education of the Gifted, 16,* 103–19.

Armstrong, T. (1987). *In their own way.* Los Angeles: Jeremy P. Tarcher.

Association for Supervision and Curriculum Development. (1997). *Differentiating instruction.* Alexandria, VA: ASCD (video staff development set).

Austin, A. B., & Draper, D. C. (1981). Peer relationships of the academically gifted: A review. *Gifted Child Quarterly, 25*(3), 129–34.

Bacharach, N., Hasslen, R., & Anderson, J. (1995). *Learning together: A manual for multiage grouping.* Thousand Oaks, CA: Corwin Press.

Baker, J. A. (1996). Everyday stressors of academically gifted adolescents. *Journal of Secondary Gifted Education, 7,* 356–68.

Banks, C., & Banks, J. (1993). Equity pedagogy: An essential component of multicultural education. *Theory into Practice, 34*(3), 152–58.

Bateman, B. (1993). Learning disabilities: The changing landscape. *Journal of Learning Disabilities, 25*(1), 29–36.

Benbow, C. P. (1991). Meeting the needs of gifted students through acceleration: A neglected resource. In M. C. Wang, M. C. Reynolds, & H. J. Walberg (eds.), *Handbook of special education: Research and practice.* Vol. 4, *Emerging programs,* 23–36. Elmsford, NY: Pergamon Press.

———. (1998). Acceleration as a method for meeting the academic needs of intellectually talented children. In J. Van Tassel-Baska (ed.), *Excellence in educating gifted and talented learners,* 279–94. Denver: Love.

Bernardo, D. (1990). Competitive overdrive stalls high achieving teens. *Gifted Child Today* (May/June), 30–31.

Betts, G. T. (1986). Development of the emotional and social needs of gifted individuals. *Journal of Counseling and Development, 64,* 587–89.

Bingham, A. (1995). *Exploring the multiage classroom.* York, ME: Stenhouse.

Brophy, B. (1986). Workaholics beware: Long hours may not pay. *U.S. News and World Report* (April 7), 60.

Burns, D. D. (1980). The perfectionist's script for self-defeat. *Psychology Today* (November), 70–76.

Callahan, C., & Tomlinson, C. A. (1996). *Heterogeneity: Inclusion or delusion? Can we make academically diverse classrooms succeed?* Alexandria, VA: Association for Supervision and Curriculum Development.

Callard-Szulgit, R. (2003a). *Parenting and teaching the gifted.* Lanham, MD: Scarecrow Press.

———. (2003b). *Perfectionism and gifted children.* Lanham, MD: Scarecrow Press.

Carlson, R. (1997). *Don't sweat the small stuff . . . and it's all small stuff.* New York: Hyperion.

Chall, J. S., & Conrad, S. S. (1991). *Should textbooks challenge students? The case for easier or harder textbooks.* New York: Teachers College Press.

Cimochowski, A. (1993). *Cloze in on social studies.* New York: Berrent.

Clark, W. H., & Hankins, N. E. (1985). Giftedness and conflict. *Roeper Review, 8,* 50–53.

Cohen, L. M., & Frydenberg, E. (1996). *Coping for capable kids: Strategies for parents, teachers, and students.* Waco, TX: Prufrock Press.

Colangelo, N. (1997). Counseling gifted students: Issues and practices. In N. Colangelo & G. A. Davis (eds.), *Handbook of gifted education* (2d ed.), 353–65. Boston: Allyn & Bacon.

Cole, R. (1995). *Educating everybody's children: Diverse teaching strategies for diverse learners*. Alexandria, VA: Association for Supervision and Curriculum Development.

Coleman, R., & Gallagher, J. (1995). Appropriate differentiated services: Guides for best practices in the education of gifted children. *Gifted Child Today, 18*(5), 32–33.

Conrad, S., & Flegler, D. (1993). *Math contest: Grades 7 and 8 (and Algebra Course 1)*. Tenafly, NJ: Math League Press.

Cross, T. L. (2001). *On the social and emotional lives of gifted children*. Waco, TX: Prufrock Press.

———. (2002). Putting the well-being of all students (including gifted students) first. *Gifted Child Today*, 14–17.

Delisle, J., & Galbraith, J. (2001). *When gifted kids don't have all the answers: How to meet their social and emotional needs*. Minneapolis: Free Spirit.

Dickinson, C., Dickinson, P., & Rideout, E. (1987). *Brainstorming: Activities for creative thinking*. Palo Alto, CA: Creative Publications.

Eberle, B., & Stanish, B. (1985). *CPS for kids: A resource book*. East Aurora, NY: D.O.K. Publishers.

Ehrlich, S. (2001). *Rationales for funding gifted education*. Minneapolis: Minnesota Council for the Gifted and Talented.

Elkind, D. (1981). *The hurried child: Growing up too fast too soon*. Reading, MA: Addison-Wesley.

———. (1997). *All grown up and no place to go: Teenagers in crisis*. Reading, MA: Addison Wesley Longman.

Emmett, J., & Minor, C. (1993). Career decision-making factors in gifted young adults. *Career Development Quarterly, 41*, 350–65.

Erickson, H. (1998). *Concept-based curriculum and instruction: Teaching beyond the facts*. Newbury Park, CA: Corwin.

Feldheusen, J. F. (1989). Why the public schools will continue to neglect the gifted. *Gifted Child Today, 12*(2), 56–59.

Flanders, J. R. (1987). How much of the content in mathematics textbooks is new? *Arithmetic Teacher, 35*(1), 18–23.

Freeman, J. (1994). Some emotional aspects of being gifted. *Journal for the Education of the Gifted, 17*(2), 180–97.

Galbraith, J., & Delisle, J. (1996). *The gifted kids' survival guide: A teen handbook*. Minneapolis: Free Spirit.

Gallagher, J., & Gallagher, S. (1994). *Teaching the Gifted Child*. 4th ed. Boston: Allyn and Bacon.

Garcia, R. (1983). *Teaching in a pluralistic society*. New York: Harper & Row.

Gardner, H. (1984). *Frames of mind: The theory of multiple intelligences.* New York: Basic Books.

———. (1993). *Multiple intelligences: The theory in practice.* New York: Basic Books.

———. (1996). Are there additional intelligences? In J. Kane (ed.), *Educational information and transformation.* New York: Prentice Hall.

———. (1999). *Intelligences reframed.* New York: Basic Books.

Garland, A. F., & Zigler, E. (1999). Emotional and behavioral problems among highly intellectually gifted youth. *Roeper Review, 22,* 41–44.

Gentry, M., & Kettle, K. (1998). *Distinguishing myths from realities: NRCG/T research.* NRCG/T Winter Newsletter.

Hess, L. (1994). Life, liberty, and the pursuit of perfection. *Gifted Child Today* (May/June), 28–31.

Hipp, E. (1995a). *Fighting invisible tigers.* Minneapolis: Free Spirit.

———. (1995b). *Fighting invisible tigers: A stress management guide for teens.* Minneapolis: Free Spirit.

Karnes, F., & Marquardt, R. (1991). *Gifted children and the law: Mediation, due process, and court cases.* Dayton: Ohio Psychology Press.

Karnes, F., & Marquardt, R. (eds.). (1991). *Gifted children and legal issues in education: Parents' stories of hope.* Dayton: Ohio Psychology Press.

Kerr, B. (1991). *A handbook for counseling the gifted and talented.* Alexandria, VA: American Counseling Association.

———. (1996). *Smart girls, women and giftedness.* Phoenix: Great Potential Press.

———. (1997). *Smart girls: A new psychology of girls, women, and giftedness.* Scottsdale, AZ: Gifted Psychology Press.

Kerr, B., & Cohn, S. (2001). *Smart boys: Talent, manhood, and the search for meaning.* Phoenix: Great Potential Press.

Khatena, J. (1982). *Educational psychology of the gifted.* New York: Wiley.

Killion, J., NSDC, and NEA. (2003). *Results-based staff development for the middle school: What works in the middle, what works in the elementary grades, what works in the high school.* Denver: National Staff Development Council.

Landrum, M., Callahan, C., & Shaklee, B. (2001). *Aiming for excellence: Gifted program standards.* Waco, TX: Prufrock Press.

Leman, K. (1985). *The birth order book: Why you are the way you are.* New York: Dell.

Lightcap, S. J. (1985). *The dark side of giftedness.* ERIC Document Reproduction Service No. ED260529.

Mackinnon, D. W. (1978). *In search of human effectiveness: Identifying and developing creativity*. Buffalo, NY: Creative Education Foundations.

Maeda, B. (1994). *The multiage classroom: An inside look at a community of learners*. Cypress, CA: Creative Teaching Press.

Maker, C. J., Nielson, A. B., & Rogers, J. A. (1994). Multiple intelligences, giftedness, diversity, and problem-solving. *Teaching Exceptional Children, 27* (1), 4–19.

Mastropieri, M. A., & Scruggs, T. E. (2002). *Effective instruction for special education*. 3d ed. Austin, TX: Pro-Ed.

Moon, S. M., Kelly, K. R., & Feldhusen, J. F. (1997). Specialized counseling services for gifted youth and their families: A needs assessment. *Gifted Child Quarterly, 41*, 16–25.

NAGC. (1998). Pre-K–grade 12 gifted standards, 5. In *Gifted education programming criterion: Socio-emotional guidance and counseling*.

Nugent, S. A. (2002). Perfectionism: Its manifestations and classroom-based interventions. *Journal of Secondary Gifted Education, 11*, 215–21.

Parker, W. D., & Mills, C. J. (1996). The incidence of perfectionism in gifted children. *Gifted Quarterly, 40*, 194–99.

Piechowski, M. M. (1997). Developmental potential. In N. Colangelo & R. T. Zaffran (eds.), *New voice in counseling the gifted*, 25–27. Dubuque, IA: Kendall/Hunt.

Pufal-Struzik, I. (1999). Self-actualization and other personality dimensions and predictors of mental health of intellectually gifted students. *Roeper Review, 22*, 44–47.

Reis, S. M. (1994). How schools are shortchanging the gifted. *Technology Review, 97*(3), 38–45.

———. (1995). Providing equity for all: Meeting the needs of high-ability students. In H. Pool & J. A. Page (eds.), *Beyond tracking: Finding success in inclusive schools*, 119–31. Bloomington, IN: Phi Delta Kappa.

Reis, S. M., Burns, D. E., & Renzulli, J. S. (1992). *Curriculum compacting: The complete guide to modifying the regular curriculum for high-ability students*. Mansfield Center, CT: Creative Learning Press.

Reis, S. M., Westberg, J., Kulikowich, J., Caillard, F., Hebert, T., Purcell, J. H., Rogers, J., Swist, J., & Plucker, J. (1992). *An analysis of curriculum compacting on classroom practices: Technical report*. Storrs, CT: National Research Center on the Gifted and Talented.

Rimm, S. B. (1993). Gifted kids have feelings, too. *Gifted Child Today* (January/February), 20–24.

Robinson, A. (1990). Point-counterpoint: Cooperation or exploitation? The argument against cooperative learning for talented students. *Journal for the Education of the Gifted, 14*, 9–27.

Ross, P. (ed.). (1993). *National excellence: A case for developing America's talent.* Washington, DC: U.S. Department of Education.

Schwartz, L. L. (1994). Educating the gifted to the gifted: A national resource. In *Why give "gifts" to the gifted? Investing in a national resource,* 1–7. Thousands Oaks, CA: Corwin Press.

Shroeder, D. S. (1994). Giftedness: A double-edged sword. *Book Links* (March), 25.

Stainback, W., & Stainback, S. (1994). *Curriculum considerations in inclusive classrooms: Facilitating learning for all students.* Maryland Heights, MO: Paul H. Brooks.

Sternberg, R. (1997). What does it mean to be smart? *Educational Leadership,* 54(6), 20–24.

Terman, L. M. (1947). *Mental and physical traits of a thousand gifted children.* Vol. 1, *Genetic studies of genius.* Stanford, CA: Stanford University Press.

Tomlinson, C. (1995). *How to differentiate instruction in mixed-ability classrooms: A professional inquiry kit.* Alexandria, VA: Association for Supervision and Curriculum Development.

———. (1999). *The differentiated classroom: Responding to the needs of all learners.* Alexandria, VA: Association for Supervision and Curriculum Development.

Treffinger, D. J., Callahan, C., & Baughn, V. L. (1991). Research on enrichment efforts in gifted education. In M. C. Wang, M. C. Reynolds, & H. J. Walberg (eds.), *Handbook of special education: Research and practice.* Vol. 4, *Emerging programs,* 37–55. Oxford: Pergamon Press.

Usiskin, Z. (1987). Why elementary algebra can, should, and must be an eighth-grade course for average students. *Mathematics Teacher,* 80(6), 428–38.

Weisse, D. (1990). Gifted adolescents and suicide. *School Counselor, 37,* 351–57.

Whitmore, A. (1980). *Giftedness, conflict, and underachievement.* Needham Heights, MA: Allyn & Bacon.

Winebrenner, S. (1992). *Teaching gifted kids in the regular classroom.* Minneapolis: Free Spirit.

———. (1996). *Teaching kids with learning difficulties in the regular classroom.* Minneapolis: Free Spirit.

Winner, E. (1996). *Gifted children: Myths and realities.* New York: Basic Books.

ABOUT THE AUTHOR

Dr. Rosemary Callard-Szulgit is the author of two very successful books published in 2003: *Parenting and Teaching the Gifted* and *Perfectionism and Gifted Children*. She is an associate professor at the State University of New York, College at Brockport, where her courses "Teaching the Gifted, K–12," "Teaching Writing, K–12," and "Teaching Reading, K–12" have become highly respected. Rosemary is also the former facilitator for gifted and talented, K–8, in the Webster Central School District in a large suburb of Rochester, New York.

Recognized in *Who's Who among American Educators*, Rosemary brings 37 years of research and classroom experiences in elementary, middle school, and university settings to her role as an author and staff development trainer of parents, teachers, and children throughout the country.

Rosemary has spoken at the First United States–China Conference on Education, in Beijing, and has presented for the American Creativity Association, National Association for Gifted, World Council on Gifted, West Virginia Annual Reading Conference, and United States–Russia Conference on Education, as well as consulting throughout the United States. She continues to have articles published dealing with the education of gifted children and will have her fourth book, *Math and Science Activities for the Gifted*, published in 2005.

Rosemary's staff development consulting business, Partners for Excellence, in Rochester, New York, may be accessed on the Internet at www.partners-for-excellence.com.